"Tim Soerens believes that when flourishing networks of churches care about their neighborhoods, seeking the shalom of everyone and everything there, they form the connective tissue that brings hope and healing to our divided society. And when you read how he describes this wonderful task, you'll believe it too. This book is tender and rousing in equal measure."

Michael Frost, author of *To Alter Your World* and *Incarnate*

"By reminding us of God's big dream, Tim sheds new light on evangelism, discipleship, and the missional purpose of the people of God. I'm excited about getting this resource into the hands of our ministry influencers."

Al Engler, associate field director with the Navigators

"As I read, I felt my heart racing with two possibilities: 'I'm not alone!' and 'What seems like church meltdown could be the stirring of new movement!' Many conversations about the church talk about it in third person, as if it's an institution to fix. Tim Soerens invites us to name the often unspoken emotional and cultural realities at work in our own human hearts that prompt us to be part of the problem. With pastoral patience he speaks to the discouraged, grieving, anxious, frustrated church, calling us to become Christ's humble, peaceful, prayerful, attentive, curious, hopeful church, one reader at a time."

Mandy Smith, pastor and author of *The Vulnerable Pastor*

"Tim Soerens looks at the world not through rose-colored glasses but through God's eyes. He invites us to see the color and wonder and life that is bursting out all around us, often in unexpected places."

Michael Mather, author of *Having Nothing, Possessing Everything: Finding Abundant Communities in Unexpected Places*

"*Everywhere You Look* is a refreshing reminder of the need to refocus our energy on the heart of God. Using theological and practical insight that challenges us all, this book pushes us to see the current polarized climate of the church as an opportunity rather than an obstacle. Tim Soerens gives us a glimpse into what is possible if we open our eyes to what God is already doing, beginning right where we are."

Jonathan F   munity Church, Chicago

"If you have left the church, if you are thinking about leaving your fellowship, or if you are thinking about becoming a part of Christ's body, STOP! You should read *Everywhere You Look* by Tim Soerens as the next step of your journey. This book, written by someone who has been in your shoes, is not another formula or fad but has a way of answering all the questions you forgot to ask. Soerens presents a uniquely uncomplicated way forward for the body of Christ, and in our present dilemma, that is an extraordinary gift!"

Randy Woodley, activist-scholar and farmer, author of *Living in Color*

"With this book, Tim Soerens sets us on a journey to reexamine 'Why church?' A manifest plea to all who are ready to give up on church, *Everywhere You Look* invites us to find new practices, pray with new fervor, and embrace a new church emerging all around us. Reading it will force you to think, imagine, and do new things."

David Fitch, Lindner Chair of Evangelical Theology at Northern Seminary Chicago, author of *Faithful Presence*

"*Everywhere You Look* is the manifesto on church and community I have been waiting for. Revolutionary in its simplicity and pulsing with possibility, this book got its hooks in me and won't let go. "God is up to something," Soerens writes. May our dusty ideas and duct-taped plans crumble as we wake up, link arms, and head out to the streets to see it for ourselves."

Shannan Martin, author of *The Ministry of Ordinary Places* and *Falling Free*

"Tim expresses the radical notion that church should be not just a place but a way of living out loud while paying attention to those around you. This book is a meditation on inspiring neighbors to see God's love in action through our actions."

Majora Carter, urban revitalization strategist and broadcast producer/host from the South Bronx, New York City

"Tim Soerens delightfully invites us to experience and engage the love of God in our neighborhoods, helping us discover what it means to be the church in our everyday lives and places. We need these stories and guiding practices, perhaps more than ever! This book illuminates a true revival for the future of the chruch."

Christiana Rice, coauthor of *To Alter Your World: Partnering with God to Rebirth Our Communities*

EVERYWHERE YOU LOOK

DISCOVERING THE CHURCH RIGHT WHERE YOU ARE

TIM SOERENS

FOREWORD BY
WALTER BRUEGGEMANN

An imprint of InterVarsity Press
Downers Grove, Illinois

InterVarsity Press
P.O. Box 1400, Downers Grove, IL 60515-1426
ivpress.com
email@ivpress.com

InterVarsity Press® is the book-publishing division of InterVarsity Christian Fellowship/USA®, a movement of students and faculty active on campus at hundreds of universities, colleges, and schools of nursing in the United States of America, and a member movement of the International Fellowship of Evangelical Students. For information about local and regional activities, visit intervarsity.org.

Scripture quotations, unless otherwise noted, are from the New Revised Standard Version of the Bible, copyright 1989 by the Division of Christian Education of the National Council of the Churches of Christ in the USA. Used by permission. All rights reserved.

While any stories in this book are true, some names and identifying information may have been changed to protect the privacy of individuals.

Published in association with the literary agency of D.C. Jacobson & Associates, an Author Management Company. http://www.dcjacobson.com.

Figures 2.1, 2.2, 3.1, 3.2, 4.1, 5.1, 6.1, 7.1, and 8.2 by Coté Soerens.

Cover design and image composite: David Fassett
Interior design: Daniel van Loon
Images: abstract color shapes © CSA Images / Getty Images
   star illustration © CSA Images / Getty Images
   leafy plant illustration © CSA Images / Getty Images

ISBN 978-0-8308-4156-1 (print)
ISBN 978-0-8308-4196-7 (digital)

Printed in the United States of America ♾

InterVarsity Press is committed to ecological stewardship and to the conservation of natural resources in all our operations. This book was printed using sustainably sourced paper.

Library of Congress Cataloging-in-Publication Data
A catalog record for this book is available from the Library of Congress.

P   25 24 23 22 21 20 19 18 17 16 15 14 13 12 11 10 9 8 7 6 5 4 3 2 1

Y   38 37 36 35 34 33 32 31 30 29 28 27 26 25 24 23 22 21 20

For Lukas and Joaquín, with all my love

CONTENTS

FOREWORD

Walter Brueggemann

Tim Soerens has written a passionate book concerning the future of the church. To his writing he brings his years of street smarts about how communities work. His book is both deeply grounded in vigorous *theological claims* and wisely alert in *practical matters*. He begins his account of the church with a stark either-or: either *institutional decay* or vibrant *movement*. It does not take long for him to dispose of the status quo as a viable option. While the institutional church is needed, its heavy burden of nostalgia, default to quick fixes, and shrinking budgets will necessarily require new imagination. Any church is headed for meltdown that has become an end in itself, preoccupied with survival and therefore growth.

It is, however, the other side of that either-or that concerns Soerens and that will be the hope-filled future of the church, namely, to recover its authentic character as a movement of

1

God's Spirit toward an alternative life in the world. In his transition from theology to practice, Soerens begins by asking the "big why" question: Why a church at all? The answer is that the church's *why* is found in God's desire to which we may attach our own desire. That desire of God is that the world be a venue of generous neighborliness. The church exists to embrace the desire of God!

That embrace of God's desire, however, is not simply a task to be performed by our best effort and commitment. Much beyond our best effort and commitment, we are invited to notice what God's own Spirit is doing in the world, nothing less than "deconstructing and obstructing our contemporary towers" of pride, greed, and control. Soerens sees quite clearly that God's Spirit is actively and assertively countercultural. In a world of fear, greed, and hostility, the Spirit is working otherwise to make room for peaceable generosity that runs beyond our own capacity.

The truth of the *big why* and the *countercultural work of the Spirit* provides the foundation for communities of faith that sign on for the *why* and the *work* that counter the fear and greed of the world. By appeal to the verdict that "the neighborhood is the unit of change," Soerens morphs to "the parish is the unit of change." Of course, by *parish* he does not refer to the failed local congregations that remain stuck in rote performances that endlessly reiterate and refuse newness. He refers, rather, to "the new parish" that is both large enough to live life together and small enough to be known in honest engagement. While he does not acknowledge it, he would surely recognize that many old parishes are already bent toward the new parish and include energized folk who are living together in loving

2

and joyous missional engagement. Thus the new parish model may take heart because there are already many venues of fresh articulation and fresh courage for a way ahead. It might be recognized that Soerens, given his ecclesial background, continues to have one eye on mega-congregations that are much too often focused on growth, power, and wealth. But of course Soerens knows as well many other congregations that live much closer to the *why* of God.

The remainder of Soerens's fine work is a reflection on the life of the right-sized parish that takes the form of a team that is deeply committed not only to the mission but whose members are deeply committed to each other for a common life of trust, joy, and honesty. His sketch of such a new parish is reminiscent of the early church in the book of Acts in which the members had "all things in common." Soerens does not focus on shared economics, but a fully shared life will, perforce, have economic implications. He articulates a suggestive taxonomy of a team of engaged people who live at the center of a parish. Though all the members of the parish are not fully on board with the team, they may and will be drawn toward the vision of such an intentional group. That performed vision, powered by the Spirit, will, he suggests, not only reach the larger church but the civic community as well.

Everyone knows it is a hard time for the church in our culture, a hard time reflected for Soerens in secular Seattle as his home base. Much of that hard time, of course, results from the church having forgotten its character and purpose. In the face of that hard time, Soerens has written a book that teems with hope and possibility for the future, a *hope* that the church need not reiterate our mistaken past, and a *possibility* that real people in real time and real circumstance can live out the *why* of God. The prospect Soerens explores is of a community of glad neighborliness in which faithful folk genuinely delight in one another and happily share a vision of a world that is engaged by the Spirit. Soerens finishes with a judgment that the most elemental need for the church is passionate prayer whereby we put "ourselves in the rightful posture that we cannot control the outcomes we seek." I finished reading the book with exhilaration for what lies ahead for the church. Now is no time for regret or anxiety. Now is a time for recovery of the newness of what is old and best in our tradition. Soerens brings his great lived wisdom to his exposition, a practical wisdom whereby we may be instructed. In the new parish there will be no business as usual, but a glad return to the grit and energy of the apostles.

CHAPTER ONE

THE MOVEMENT OR
THE MELTDOWN

Claudette Colvin doesn't have any museums or holidays named after her, but she should. You've undoubtedly heard of Rosa Parks, the young woman who was ruthlessly dragged off a bus in Montgomery, Alabama, for refusing to give her seat to a white person. What many people don't know is that nine months earlier the same thing happened to Claudette. On March 15, 1955, on her way home from high school, fifteen-year-old Claudette took a seat on a bus in Montgomery. When the bus driver told her to give her seat to a white person, she refused. Within minutes her books were flying in the air; two police officers put her in handcuffs and started to drag her off the bus. Without fighting back or cussing, she kept telling everyone who would listen that sitting on the bus was her constitutional right, but that didn't keep her from ending up in the adult jail at the police station. While in lockup, she prayed the Lord's Prayer and Psalm 23 over and over, all the while hoping her family and neighbors would somehow discover she was there. She hadn't been given the opportunity to call anyone. Thankfully, her schoolmates who were also on the bus spread the word around the neighborhood.

Mary Ann Colvin, Claudette's mom, was a maid who took care of three other children in their neighborhood. Once word spread of what had happened to Claudette, a few nearby girls scurried over to watch the kids while Mary Ann frantically thought about how to get to the police station. She hastily called Claudette's pastor, the Reverend H. H. Johnson, who had a car, and together they raced to the police station. Rev. Johnson was able to bail out Claudette and told her, "Claudette, I'm so proud of you. Everyone prays for freedom. We've all been praying and praying. But you're different—you want your answer the next morning. And I think you just brought the revolution to Montgomery."[1]

Most people don't know Claudette's name, but that doesn't change the fact that her grit and resolve cultivated the soil for moments like the Montgomery Bus Boycott, Dr. King's legendary speeches, and the signing of the Civil Rights Act in 1963. She is an icon to me because her courage was on display at the moment before the movement. She knew she had the support of her family and neighborhood, but she couldn't have known at the time that her courageous action would multiply throughout the country into an unstoppable movement. It took tremendous grit not to give up her seat. With all of the stares and contempt on that bus, she must have *felt* completely alone—but she *knew* she was not alone.

History has a way of remembering the icons, the ones who seemingly spark a movement from thin air, but of course this is never the case. There is no isolated genius. We should keep celebrating the major breakthroughs of history: Rosa Parks' arrest, the "I Have a Dream" speech of Dr. King, the passing of landmark legislation. It's pretty standard to remember major historical movements by marking the day or celebrating the person who embodies that final climactic moment of victory. But increasingly I find myself even more inspired by what happened before the breakthrough. What are the common themes of these crucial moments before the movement? Might there be clues for us to discern whether something much larger is happening around us today?

I'm not a historian, but it seems to me that before any major movement, before any history-making transition, a few common traits emerge. Right before most movements, the following almost always occur:

✦ People are afraid to ask out loud big, important questions.

✦ Polarization and a sense of nostalgia escalate.

✦ Disconnected grassroots experiments take place on the margins.

Before the movement there are sustained moments when all feels lost, when something feels impossibly broken, when confusion and fragmentation seem to be the norm. A hazy cloud of anxiety seems to pervade the lives of more and more everyday people. We want to know if we're the only ones asking these questions, having these doubts, longing for reasons to hope.

Does this sound familiar? Are we closer to a breakthrough movement or have we just begun the meltdown? In most of the headlines about the church right now, it feels a lot more like we are approaching a meltdown.

Beneath the surface of our perplexing cultural moment, Christians from all sorts of backgrounds are wondering what is going on. A creeping suspicion has been growing for years that maybe things are getting worse. Polarization is exploding, isolation is pervasive, and this is all happening as the new millennial generation, with a historically poor attitude toward institutions, is coming of age. There is well-documented and understandable suspicion of large corporations, exhaustion from our polarized national government, and lack of participation in associations. It can feel like we are in the midst of a great unraveling or, as writer George Packer calls it, "the unwinding."[2] In this era of confusion many of our institutions are tempted by former glories of the past rather than risking a bold new future. This is true of many of our churches as well.

As more and more everyday people struggle to hope, those of us following Jesus must ask, How do we embody news that is so good it draws the attention and longing of our neighbors? At the moment when so many of our neighbors seem to be most in need of a local church, do we have the imagination and clarity of vision to answer the ancient call to be the people of God who are blessed to be a blessing (see Genesis 12:2-3)?

The truth is that at the very moment when the strong social fabric of love and care is so desperately needed, we most often hear that the church is dying. It seems like every month a new celebrity pastor flames out. We read about congregations that appear more aligned with a particular political party than the redemptive story of God. We drive by dozens of church buildings that are empty or have been ignored for decades.

No wonder a growing industry of books and conferences on post-Christian America fearfully predicts the death of the church as we know it. I believe many of these forecasts to be true, but I increasingly find myself captivated by a simple idea. What if our inherited imagination of what the church should be is dying while the Spirit is stirring up something new?

We are either in the moment before the meltdown or a new movement. This book is a guide to see what's possible and to build momentum toward a movement I believe is already underway. I'm convinced that God is asking us to embrace this season as an unprecedented opportunity. At a time when everything seems to be getting more confusing, clarity is emerging for how we can be the church in our everyday lives together.

We won't yet read about these growing experiments from the headlines. We can't get there from the normal pathways. But if we join together in planting our feet on the ground, I think we just might see a history-making opportunity to join God in transforming how everyday people experience the church. *More than changing what we do, we first need to change how we see.* I have personally witnessed ordinary heroes like Claudette Colvin in just about every neighborhood I've had the honor of exploring. Thousands of courageous Christians are trying new things, taking new risks, and answering the ancient call to be God's people on behalf of others. But if we are going to have the eyes to see them, we must question our default settings in how we pay attention to God at work in our everyday lives and how we have been conditioned to view the church as a timebound and static event.

The Secret on the Street

Along with some incredible colleagues, I've been privileged to spend the past ten years in hundreds of neighborhoods listening to stories of hope. I've sat in dark pubs late at night and in bright kitchens at the crack of dawn. Over the years I've slept on more couches than I care to count. My travels have taken me to gritty urban neighborhoods, cozy suburban towns, and tranquil rural villages. I've talked to trust-fund hipsters, Black Lives Matter activists, self-described rednecks, accomplished scholars in their eighties, and idealistic teenagers. Hopeful stories of transformation are popping up everywhere as ordinary people discern what it could mean to be the church in everyday life. A groundswell of momentum is gaining traction just in time to counter our cultural moment of fragmentation and confusion.

If you doubt me, I can't blame you. After all, religious journalists won't cover most of these stories because they don't know where to look. Most pastors won't see it because they're focused on their own congregations. To witness what's actually happening, we need to walk a few streets, ask plenty of questions, and be on the lookout for what God is doing in our everyday lives. If we look at the headlines, all we see is meltdown; when we get on the street it feels more like a movement.

We are at a tipping point for the church, at least for the church in North America. In all sorts of environments, when I have asked people about what the church or its purpose is, I've gotten such diverse answers that I wonder if the practical imagination of the church is essentially up for grabs. On the one hand, millions of mostly young people are giving up on the church. It just doesn't make sense to them, and as a result they are placing their attention, hope, and time where they believe more change can happen. On the other hand is a movement that sounds an awful lot like "Make the Church Great Again." But, both of these impulses make a profound mistake in *asking questions about the church before asking questions about what God is doing*. Ironically, the more obsessively we focus on the church, the harder it is to focus on God, who is making all things new and is active in our everyday lives.

When I say the experience of church is up for grabs, I'm not talking about how we feel when we attend a Sunday gathering. I'm talking about how everyday people imagine what the church is all about. From conservative evangelical churches in small Midwestern towns to mainline churches in bustling San Francisco, from two hundred-year-old establishments in New York to two-month-old church plants in New Mexico, a crucial question is rising: Rather than occasionally attend a service, how do we become the visible body of Christ in our everyday lives? I'm convinced God is prompting us to ask this question as well.

We are being shaken up to follow God into a bold new future where our faith guides our entire lives. It shapes our neighborhoods, cultivates an entirely new imagination for how we live, and draws us together when everything else seems to be tearing us apart.

How Movements Happen

Those who don't believe this transformation is possible might be in the majority. But let's consider how movements usually happen. First, the movements that matter almost always feel impossible until they aren't. Here's what I mean: the reason we don't believe change can happen is not that we don't want it and usually not because we fear something new, but because we believe that we are alone. We feel like we are the slightly crazy ones. We can see a path forward, but we don't think it's going to be possible to get there on our own. So we continue on as best we can. We know there must be something more but can't quite name it. Maybe we try some new experiments and learn from them. Often, we feel like we are on to something but wonder if we can keep going. Most of the time it feels like our families, our institutions, or even our circle of friends don't quite get it. But we carry on until one of two options presents itself. The first is to simply give up. The experiments stop; we conclude we had some great ideas and strong convictions, but we just can't keep going. It's time to fold. The cards were not in our favor. This is incredibly sad and always carries with it a sense of resignation, a tinge of bitterness, and constant second-guessing. We tell ourselves we tried, which is all we can do. It's the end, and we need to face reality. Maybe the cynics were right.

But sometimes when we are pushing toward something new we receive the gift of a new connection, and it changes everything.

It can feel like winning the lottery. It's a little disorienting because of how common and ordinary it actually is, but immediately we feel the possibility of transformation. We meet someone who has a common conviction and has courageously stepped into an experiment of their own. When we meet them, it feels like magic. Maybe we aren't so crazy after all. Maybe there is something to this! Maybe we are on the front end of a long line of innovators. As it relates to our dreams for the church, maybe God is actually doing something. Maybe seeds of discontent and desire have been planted throughout the world, and we are now starting to see the seedlings emerge from the broken soil. All of this leads to a key principle at the heart of this book: *movements happen when people who thought they were alone discover they are not.*

This principle is true in nearly every major revolution, every major transition, perhaps every significant moment that changes history. We think it's impossible because we think we are alone, but everything changes when we realize that's not true. That same desire within us to follow Jesus with our whole life, to love our actual neighbors, and to belong to a team of people in our everyday lives guided by the Great Commandment to love God and our neighbors is shared by millions. This longing might be completely unique in a particular context but is actually shared by a mostly invisible movement that hasn't been connected. What if this desire is being nurtured and cultivated by the living Spirit of God, but we all think we are alone? What if we are surrounded by ordinary saints whose deepest desire for their lives is to answer the prayer "your kingdom come, in my neighborhood as it is in heaven," but we all feel like Claudette Colvin—alone on a bus?

The Good News of Church Decline

We just might be in the early days of a reformation that will one day be written about in history books. And even if this doesn't transpire, at least we should know we are not alone. Please keep in mind that if the same driving desire within us—the fraying thread of hope that feels like it's splitting and popping with every passing day—is connected with others, it has the potential to be a strong, rich, colorful fabric of love and care in our neighborhoods. The strength of what is possible hinges on our capacity to connect.

What's at stake is not simply a *spiritual* opportunity. Our neighborhoods and cities are at stake too. At stake is the kind of businesses and economies we are going to create. What sorts of places will we design and build? How will we re-create our collective care for our kids? How will we reshape education? How will we confront the most horrific injustices of racism, sexual exploitation, and environmental abuse?

The future is at stake.

To become the church in everyday life is not a nice idea for religious people. It's a call for holistic revolution. Our gatherings, our liturgies, and our sermons will remain vital, but not if they are not oriented toward forming us to be the body of Christ in the everyday life of our neighborhoods. We must go on a journey together to recover how to be the church in our actual lives because if we don't, another story will ultimately win the day.

We believe following Jesus is the best way to live because we believe he embodies the best story. This story is not just good news for us but for our neighbors, our families, and our enemies. We are called to live out this good-news story not as isolated, well-meaning individuals but as a team that is publicly encountered in the ordinary context of particular places. If the only place our neighbors can experience the body of Christ is during our worship services, we have failed. The only viable way we can invite people to experience the good news of the gospel is by displaying a real community of people in a real place—this is the ancient practice God is calling forth in our new day. It's not a new vision, but it will require a new imagination because we live in a new moment. The only viable and enduring form of Christian witness is a community living in a particular place, and this means we need each other.

You Can't Give Up Just Yet

If you are about to give up on the church, I beg you to consider that your frustration and confusion can become the fuel of a light that could shine all over the world. God might want to use this frustration in ways we simply cannot yet imagine. In ten years—or twenty or fifty—much could be written about this exact moment, and your frustration with the church is a crucial part of the story.

God is up to something. We are blessed to live in profoundly interesting and tumultuous times. Let's figure out how to go on this journey together. Let's have the courage to imagine what sort of church we will pass on to our kids and grandkids and great-grandkids. In this cultural moment when it feels as if it takes all of our energy to get through the day, when we are constantly reacting to this or that Tweet or headline, let's focus on what is possible in a year or two or ten.

The instinct in tumultuous times like these is to double down on the demonstrable. We are tempted to capitulate to the old, false measure of buildings and budgets. The pressure that comes from most leadership teams and denominational structures is to fix the problem of attendance as soon as possible. The instinct to quickly grow attendance makes perfect emotional sense, but it could not be a worse idea. We are being called to a different challenge—a different game. We are being asked by the living God to collectively embody good news in our everyday lives. Just as most teams require huddles and time-outs, how we nurture our team will require gatherings, but for God's sake that is not the game.

Don't listen to the anxious noise. Don't believe the lie that the future of the church depends on more hype, more professionals, and more stagecraft. I've been to enough neighborhoods to tell you that *presence* trumps performance every single time.

Words Create Worlds

In college I majored in rhetoric. While this might explain why I've never had a "real" job, it also instilled in me a profound curiosity about the reality that "words create worlds." In a very real sense, the language of our everyday life actually cultivates and makes possible how we see the world, which naturally affects how we live. So, as someone who's called to give my life to the future of the church—and who cares about words and language—I'm particularly passionate about how everyday people use and misuse the word *church*.

This became apparent when my son Lukas was about two years old. He seemed to be expanding his vocabulary every week, and as a result his sweet little world was growing. One day a simple thought struck me. It was so piercing it demanded an immediate parental summit with my wife. What world would be created if Lukas grew up thinking about the word *church* as I was taught? As you can imagine, this required a strategic meeting of the highest order.

After passionately making my case and some pretty hila-
rious back and forth, it was settled. We agreed that in our home,
to the extent possible we would never allow our precious Lukas
to utter the phrase "going to church." He could say going to a
church *building*, attending a church *program*, or participating
in a church *gathering*. In his mind it would be impossible to go
to something he already belongs to. He would not confuse
identity with participation.

We go to concerts and baseball games and picnics. We don't
say when we are in this place that we are the baseball team. No,
it's something we attend. But we cannot attend something that
we, along with others, indeed have already become: the church.

Somehow, over the course of a few generations, our language has crystalized into a betrayal of the word. Of course, we
go to gatherings, we attend services, and programs require our
involvement. These are important, but we need to ask what
they are for. We can't keep calling what happens within the
church building as the entire thing itself. We blunt and min-
imize the powerful potential of the local church by turning it
into a commodity purchased with our attendance at an event.
We simply can't keep allowing our language to betray us, because our words create our worlds.

So, what world do I want my son to grow up in? I bet it's a
lot closer to what you want and what God wants as well. I want
Lukas to grow up thinking that the word *church* means a ragtag
community of men, women, and children who are more like
uncles, aunts, and cousins than awkwardly friendly strangers
in a religious building. I want him to see the church as a
movement with an ancient history and a promising future. I
want him to make the connection between the messy and

beautiful shared life of these aunts and uncles in the neighborhood as the key to understanding what the gospel of Jesus looks like. I want him to be swept up in the stream of a tangible community in his everyday life that prioritizes justice and creativity and resilience. Essentially, I want Lukas to be surrounded by people who want to follow Jesus with their entire lives and love their neighbors as themselves.

What would happen if he grew up with a group of friends determined to welcome others, to have a special concern for our neighbors who are suffering, a team relying on God to make our neighborhood whole again? A neighborhood full of life, beauty, welcome, and people who understand that their own transformation is inextricably bound up with the transformation of their neighbors? Effectively, I want him surrounded by people of hope. I desperately want that for your kids, for your grandkids, and for you as well.

This vision should not be viewed as "out there" or unusual or even particularly innovative. Shouldn't our dream be that our kids grow up thinking, acting, living, and speaking of this vision of the church as obvious and ordinary? Isn't this the view that we should hold as well?

This is not some crazy, cutting-edge vision of the church. It's simply who we are. It is also who we are called to be. We need this now more than ever. The good news is that God is calling us to become this kind of people—now. I believe that God is building this movement; *we just need to be able to see it.*

All Is Gift

If we accept the joy and burden of transforming how our neighbors and we experience what it means to be the church in our everyday lives, it won't be manufactured by flawless execution. If we are willing to reclaim God's call to be disciples of Jesus with our whole lives, we need to name our dependence on the living God upfront. If we have the audacity to chart a path that could make history, it will not be our own doing. It's critical to say upfront that this transformation we seek is a gift to be received by our active God, not a technique to be mastered by driven people. Our future will hinge on this reality. Renewal movements throughout church history have always been led by ordinary people who are so desperate for change that they forfeit their capacity to make it happen in their own power. If we become the kind of people who simultaneously pray and hope desperately for change while refusing to control the outcomes, we will be astounded at what we get to experience.

When this happens, we will say that we got to be a part of what God was doing in our day. We will tell stories to our kids, our grandkids, and our great-grandkids about God's prevailing work among the confusion of the early twenty-first century. When we look back, we will be overcome with gratitude, not pride. We will shake our heads in wonder. Our creased faces will smile in appreciation. Our tired bodies will hold within them hundreds of stories. When we look back, we will know we took the chance to partner with what God was doing in our day.

That's all coming—but first we need to look forward and have the courage to ask some hard questions. We need to uncover the hidden forces that keep us from being what we are called to become. We need to be honest with how most people experience the church and wrestle with what its purpose is, what it exists for.

We are either in the moment before the movement or the meltdown. Our present future has so much at stake. Everywhere we look God is doing a new thing in our day, and we get to receive this as the gift that it is.

CHAPTER TWO

THE BIG WHY

Not everything that is faced can be changed.
But nothing can be changed until it is faced.

JAMES BALDWIN

I grew up in a lovely household. We lived in a small Midwestern town beside a large lake. At the turn of the twentieth century, a large paper company was formed in town and grew so quickly that it put the town on the map. It was charming if fairly predictable. I had a paper route and a loyal golden retriever and loved playing basketball because of Michael Jordan. Get a feel? Small town, middle class, and, I forgot to say, evangelical. I know that word has taken on all sorts of bizarre connotations in the past few years, particularly with the Trump Administration, but essentially it meant the Bible is important, Jesus died for my sins, and for reasons I never could figure out, I wasn't allowed to watch *The Simpsons*.

So, yes, like some of you, I was formed by an intentionally Christian home. The older I get, the more grateful I am for this fact. But it was pretty immersive.

21

+ Christian grade school. *Check*
+ Attended church each Sunday. *Check*
+ Youth group on Wednesday. *Check*
+ Prayer before meals. *Check*
+ Amy Grant Christmas albums on repeat during the holiday season. *Check*

You get the idea.

When I was in about seventh grade, without too much fanfare my dad started to ask some subversive questions. This growing curiosity would have staggering implications for my family and for my own relationship with God.

I don't recall this question being posed in a dramatic family meeting. In fact, I don't think my dad ever articulated it to us kids. But it was definitely pursued with an honest and curious reverence. This question was no flippant matter. I remember it as a pursuit of God's will, even if it wasn't stated this way.

The question that kept bubbling to the surface went something like this: What is the point of the church? Why are we doing this?

We naturally take a lot of things for granted. We know that the main function of a coffee grinder is to grind coffee. The main function of this book is to be read (thanks for reading it, by the way).

So then what is the primary function of the church? What is it *for*?

This seemingly innocent question that seeped into our family has also been asked throughout church history. And it's the primary question being asked today. If you ask the question honestly, it's rarely just a question of *form*—of tweaking little things to make it better. The question that seems to fuel the dramatic exodus of all things church appears because the *functional* question is just not being answered.

There are loads of books and conversations about what happens on Sunday. In other words, here's why we should sing these songs or have the preacher talk for forty-five minutes instead of twenty-five or why we should get rid of the pews. All of these questions are legitimate, but they don't go to the underlying functional question. It's the question of purpose that sits at the center of our crisis today. Apart from church leaders, my bet is that most laypeople don't care that much about the endless experiments related to form. Millions of us —the quiet majority—are asking with sincere curiosity about the function of this thing we call the church.

Beneath much of the anxious hand-wringing of pastors, denomination leaders, consultants, conferences, and marketing tactics sits this persistently fundamental question: What is it all *for*?

Don't get me wrong; asking what the church *is*, is a big one too, but I don't believe it's quite as important. It might even be a distraction. Take for example an adjacent question like what *is* education? There is certainly a wide variety of answers to this question, and they are important. But when you ask what education is *for*, you are on a different journey. To ask what something *is* can be helpful, but it doesn't necessarily create movement, action, or change.

I'm convinced we live in an era when the foundation of much of our society is being questioned. The commonly held assumptions of why many of our institutions exist have been escalating to a tipping point of deconstruction and confusion.

When we ask what this is, we are quickly discussing philosophy, essence, or ontology (i.e., the study of being). These are fruitful questions. But when we ask what is it for? We are quickly propelled into a very different conversation.

We can do this with just about anything. What is marriage? This has been debated for a few decades now and is vitally important. But when we ask what marriage is *for*, we have a different conversation. What is business? What is business *for*? What is politics? What is politics *for*? Feel the difference?

When so much of our energy and attention is invested in fighting over what something *is*, we can actually lose sight of what it is *for*. When we play with it for a bit, it changes our posture. These questions tend to scaffold upon one another to the point that we start to ask some of the most fundamental questions we can ask of each other. Naturally, because we are seeking to be followers of Jesus, these questions must be discerned as best we can along with the living God. When Wendell Berry asks, "What are people for?" he can't answer it for himself without asking that question of God.

The little preposition *for* propels an entirely different future. When we read biographies of our heroes, we usually discover they have the courage to ask these dangerous questions of purpose. It's pretty rare for history books to be written about brave women and men who simply ask about the essence of something. History is made and change comes bounding forward when people ask these questions of purpose and answer them with their lives. Before we can grapple with our common future, we need to do our best to allow the most important questions to emerge.

A Tale of Two Questions

There is a massive disconnect I would like to try to bring to the surface. I have a hunch that it's connected to some of the confusion or angst people are experiencing in relation to the church. It's as simple as this: When I listen to most pastors, church planters, and denominational leaders, the most pervasive question I hear is, How do we fix the church? It's not usually stated so directly, but this question hovers just under the surface. It's the question beneath the question.

How do we become more relevant? Or how do we get the young people to come back? Or what do we need to do to grow? Let me be very clear, it's 100 percent understandable why these questions are frequently asked. Thousands of incredible people have accepted the call to church leadership, which is difficult, and of course their question is how do we make it better. But I don't think this question can get us where we need to go.

Underneath the massive downfall of church attendance, we've missed the mark—the question—so severely that we are at risk of losing millions more people, perhaps an entire generation or two. The question is a lot closer to what my dad asked. Why are we doing this? What is the church *for*? What is it really all about? What's the point of it? Is it simply something I grew up with? Why are there so many different kinds? Is being a part of a church community necessary to be a follower of Jesus, or is it optional?

Right now there is nothing even close to a consensus on what the church is or what it's for. In practical terms, what the church is and especially what it's for are up for grabs.

Just think for a second about how frustrating it is to be in an honest discussion (or even an argument) when neither party can seem to get on the same page regarding the question at hand. For decades an entire industry has emerged to answer the questions we are not asking, so of course we feel like we're not being heard. Of course, we tune out. Of course, we start to give up. Of course, we lose hope.

It's as if we keep asking a question, and the replies we get are comically missing the point. Just for a moment see if the following vignette rings true. (Obviously, these responses are a parody of what's happening, but take a playful posture and see if it feels like this is the conversation we keep having.)

QUESTION. What is the church for?

ANSWER. That's a good question, but maybe you didn't notice that now we can light candles and play secular music and let you talk in small groups after the sermon.

QUESTION. Yeah, but we are wrestling with what the church is for.

ANSWER. Wow, what an interesting question. Anyway, did you know our pastor is friends with Justin Bieber?

QUESTION. Seriously, we need to figure this out together. What is the church for?

ANSWER. Wow, I'm glad you feel safe to ask such important questions, but did you see that our progressive pastor has tattoos up and down her arms and casually drops the f-bomb sometimes? Isn't she so cool?

See what I mean?

I know these are silly examples, but they represent the rather ridiculous answers we keep receiving and that are making it worse. If we are going to get on the same page, it's high time we clarify what question we are starting with and go from there. If not, we risk missing each other. In fact, let's look at how these different questions invite entirely different audiences and trajectories.

Question 1. How do we fix the church?
✦ mostly asked by religious professionals
✦ points toward pastors to fix it somehow

Question 2. What is the church for?
✦ mostly asked by everyday people
✦ points toward listening to others in a context

No wonder there are days when people feel like there is no hope. I have been there myself. But I have found an oddly comforting diagram that made me feel a lot less crazy.

Three Circles Go Viral

Some people get to do TED talks because they are well known—people like Bill Gates and Sarah Silverman. Other people get the honor of doing a TED talk, and it catapults them into staggering influence. This was the case for Simon Sinek. In 2014, he did a TEDxPuget Sound talk that went viral. The first time I saw it I immediately wanted to watch it again. I had four or five ideas rushing at me all at once, and they were coming so fast I was scared that I would miss them.

Here's the big idea in a nutshell.

People don't buy *what* we are selling, they buy *why* we are selling it (see fig. 2.1). Put another way, no one buys into the idea or the hope of *what* we want to do. At a fundamental —perhaps even primal—level, it's nearly always the *why* that motivates us to take action. But here's the catch according to Sinek: we consistently talk about what we are doing, but not why. We are motivated by the why or the purpose. Once we do the hard work of clarifying the *why*, we can move on to address *how* we are going to pursue this purpose. After we have named both the why and the how, then, and only then, does it make sense to define the *what*. In the book *Start with Why*, Sinek says the "whats are important—they provide the tangible proof of the why—but why must come first. The why provides the context for everything else."[1]

Figure 2.1. Sinek's three circles

A lightbulb went off in my head that day because it gave me a frame of reference to see the mistake I was making. Without meaning to, I kept asking about the church before asking about God. The place to begin is with God, not my ideas or hopes or strategies. I kept putting the church in the center, and that is not where it belongs. In other words, I had fallen into the trap of consistently starting with the church itself and skipping God. It's a classic "savior's complex" mistake. But I don't think I'm entirely alone in this; it's possible we are accidentally reinforcing this by the way we talk with one another.

In so many of the conversations about the church, we are almost pathologically talking about what we do on Sundays. The programs we offer. What we do for kids. The time of our service. Our church or denominational tradition. Without meaning to, these conversations reinforce the idea that the purpose of the church is the church itself. When we ask what the church is for, we begin with answers about God, not just ourselves.

We now stand at a collective crossroads. Without meaning to, we have made the church itself the *why*, and it's just not working. The church alone is not a big enough container for the desires God has placed within each of us. But when we reframe the question, then we are back on track. Episcopal priest and author Fleming Rutledge says, "The calling of the church is to place itself where God is already at work."[2]

We can't make progress by asking questions about the church before we start asking questions about what God is up to, and we can't really ask questions about what God is up to without the particularity of our lives in the places we live. This is the heart of the matter. If we have the courage to continually ask what God's dreams are for our place, it creates an endless journey that requires us to listen and discern, to join and create, to ultimately receive the transformation we hope to see as a gift from the real God working in our actual lives.

My guess is that the anxiety and confusion we feel in regard to the church is wrapped up in confusing *what* with *why*. When this confusion takes hold, the implications are enormous. At stake is not just the future of the church but the future of our neighborhoods, our cities, our economies, our politics, and our families. When we confuse *what* with *why*, our future is at stake. We simply cannot confuse the two.

If we keep insisting that the church itself is the big *why*, it's only a matter of time before we embrace faddish new programs led by well-meaning religious professionals who orient their entire vocation around selling us on how cool their church is compared to that pathetic old church down the road. This is killing us. The church was never intended to be the *why*, and when we try to make it so, we lose every time. This doesn't mean it's not important or vital, but for God's actual sake we cannot keep focusing on ourselves and hope for a different result. I am convinced that the root of our problem is that we think the big *why* of the church is the church itself. However, it's not a big enough container for us.

What we focus on as our primary question will determine our entire journey. We need to wrestle through this in our actual lives, which are always embedded in everyday concrete places.

So what is our why? How do we create a clear pathway that's big enough for all of us?

The big *why* goes by plenty of names. Professors might say "eschatology." Jesus talked about "the kingdom of God." Native American brothers and sisters call it "the harmony way." The Jewish tradition directs us toward "shalom." African American resilience and vision points to "the Beloved Community." My pastor friends speak of "the reconciliation and renewal of all things." What all these terms point to is the holistic healing God is doing through Christ by the power of the Holy Spirit. This is good news for each of us. Theologian Howard Snyder says, "The gospel is about healing the disease of sin—and the healing of all creation through Jesus Christ by the Holy Spirit. Sin is the disease, salvation is the cure."[3]

I like to refer to the big *why* as "God's dream" (see fig. 2.2) because it gets at God's desire for how we should all live together and includes the nuanced reality that each of us needs salvation as well. This macrodream is huge in that it's for all people, all neighborhoods, all cities, all the land, all enemies, all of creation—everything. But it's also small in that it demonstrates God's passionate desire to be in relationship with individuals and to break down all barriers that stand between us and our beloved Creator. God also wants to heal any division within us that is stored in our individual bodies. All the shame and fear and abuse and injustices that are literally within our bodies—God wants to heal all of it if we will allow it.[4] God dreams about restoring every relationship in our families, in our marriages, in our neighborhoods, with our friends, and even with our enemies.

This breathtaking dream of healing is macro and micro, collective and individual, relational and systemic; it's all of it. It also persistently raises the question, What is God's dream for how we should live together? This is what Jesus constantly pointed to, taught about, prayed, suffered, and rose for. This is why he is our Lord and Savior. We place our trust in him because we have learned the hard way that his desires for us trump even our own. God's dream of literally

Figure 2.2. The church's why: God's dream

healing everything through Christ means there is not a molecule, relationship, or system that God does not want to restore to its gloriously created intention. When this healing dream of God is at our center, is our purpose, then the questions of the church begin to make more sense!

In essence, the healthiest, most innovative, inclusive, courageous communities of faith don't become that way by trying harder to be a great church; they get that way because they have been gripped by what God is doing, and they join in. But to get there we need to be honest about what we really want. When we wrestle with any conceivable *why*, we are addressing the issue of desire. We need to come clean with our desires and God's desires for us.

In three of the four Gospels, Jesus gets to the crux of the issue: "Those who want to save their life will lose it, and those who lose their life for my sake, and for the sake of the gospel, will save it" (Mark 8:35; Luke 9:24; John 12:25).

If we are going to experience a breakthrough, we need to have the courage to ask what God wants. To ask, "What is the desire of God?" cuts to the chase in regard to what we believe about God. Then, in the next breath we must ask, "What do we really want?" This question gets to the heart of discipleship. Few of us would say that our truest desire is to be able to comfortably check off the religion box to help get us through our week. But if that is the honest truth, it's better to start there. Why is this our greatest desire? What needs to be named and mourned and struggled with? Where have we given up a bigger, more daring dream of God's renewal in our lives? How did so many of us settle for three peppy songs, a slow one, and a feel-good message surrounded by strangers?

Just about every moment we are awake, we find things contesting for our attention and imagination, both of which cultivate our desire. The most theologically profound question we can ask ourselves is this: What do I truly want? I add the word *truly* because if we keep digging into this question, into our truest desires—the questions beneath the question—we find ourselves faced with longings and hopes planted in our souls by the living God. *What do you truly want?*

Perhaps it's too simple, but one way of thinking about spiritual formation is simply to take an honest assessment of our desires and God's desires for our life. Our desires are shaped by something. We all have a vision for the good life, and if we are not ruthlessly intentional about it, global capitalism, the American Dream of upward mobility, or some other story is quite content to give us some ideas.

Until our desires begin to overlap with God's desires for our actual lives in our actual neighborhoods, we will feel a faint and persistent ache that something is off. Even though it might hurt, this severe mercy is a gift. We are surrounded by powerful stories that tell us to "recover your authentic self" by looking inward and pursue the happiness and pleasure we deserve. God does want us to recover our true, honest, and authentic self, but not divorced from God's dream for the world.

The pinnacle of life is not becoming an influencer on Instagram or having the time and money to travel endlessly or landing the dream job. We can only find our life by losing it, by giving ourselves to God's dreams and hopes. This puzzle is at the heart of why so many of us are so anxious and depressed. Our culture tells us to live our best *individual* life; we are the center of it all. But this violates a deeper truth at the heart of all creation.

This is not something we can escape. To live is to be shaped by multiple stories competing for our deepest affections. And as the great poet, farmer, and revolutionary Wendell Berry claims, "it all turns on affection."[5] We become what we most want. Or put another way, "you are what you love."[6] Every Christ-follower is needed at this movement of becoming the church for a new day. We need to show up, and that means we need to be honest to God with our desires. We also need to be ruthless in discerning what God wants.

When our desires overlap with God's desires, we are poised for the ride of our lives. When the primary question becomes what are God's dreams for my life, for my family, for my neighborhood, then we are on the right track. We will discover the church's purpose by asking what God dreams for our place. This must always be the first question. It's the question we will keep returning to time and time again.

So, if God's dream is the big *why* at the center, what is next? How do we go about pursuing God's dream, and where in the world should this play out?

CHAPTER THREE

THE MAGIC OF PAYING ATTENTION

*Attention is the rarest and purest
form of generosity.*

Simone Weil

You know that little feeling of joy you get when you post something to Facebook or Instagram and it gets more likes than you thought it would? Okay, maybe joy is a bit of a stretch, but it feels good, right? That nice moment is brought to you by dopamine released in your brain *and* by a guy in San Francisco named Justin Rosenstein.[1] While dopamine has been called the "Kim Kardashian" of molecules because of its popularity in scientific studies, it's something we all love to feel.[2] This knowledge has fueled the user interface of so many of the apps on our phones, tablets, and computers. When technology is specifically designed to release dopamine in order to drive ad revenue, we might be in murky ethical waters.

This is where Justin Rosenstein fits in. He's the inventor of the now infamous "Like" button on Facebook. If you're anything like me, you can't even remember a time when Facebook didn't have a Like button. It seems that posting adorable pictures of your kids and seeing a rush of likes were made for each other. Well, as it turns out, they were. This loop of posting and then staying glued to our phones to see what happens initially propelled Mr. Rosenstein to Silicon Valley royalty. Now he is genuinely freaked out about what he created.

Not only can our minds be hijacked toward constantly craving another hit of dopamine, but also, as Rosenstein laments, "Everyone is distracted, all of the time."[3] A case in point: I have two little kids and work all day long, so my only window for writing is between 5 and 7 a.m., before my kids wake up. I say this because I have a limited time to focus, and while researching these articles on distraction, I found myself clicking from the helpful article in the *Guardian* to Justin Rosenstein's Twitter page to another Twitter page that was suggested, and just like that I was down the rabbit hole for ten precious minutes. And that was after two cups of coffee with a few candles flickering in the predawn darkness and a perfectly quiet home!

It's pretty clear from emerging studies and revelations by former technologists on attention that I'm not the only one who struggles with staying focused.[4] Our capacity to be fully present in any given moment is constantly under assault, and this poses a grave danger to making progress in following the way of Jesus in our everyday life. I believe Simon Sinek is right that the starting point for any major shift we make is to recover the big *why*. But I'm convinced this notion of paying attention sets the stage for *how* we go about pursuing God's dream in our neighborhoods, suburbs, and villages. The magic of paying attention to the Spirit at work in our neighborhoods is the only legitimate way forward. While that might sound bombastic, I hope it gets your attention.

Most of us were taught that once we discern the reason for something, how we get it done doesn't matter so much. After all, there are hundreds of ways to work toward something; who really cares how we do it as long as people are motivated and working toward a common goal, right? Sadly that has been the logic of nearly every colonial mission enterprise throughout history. It's a history we need to keep learning from but not repeating. We don't get divine direction and then crank it out on our own. That's precisely why our history of pursuing God's mission of redemption is riddled with violence, theft, and coercion. While there may be thousands of strategies for pursuing God's dream in all of our diverse contexts, there really is only one way forward in regard to *how* we do it—and that pathway is to listen intently and pay attention to the Holy Spirit, who is already at work.

Only One Way Forward?

Some of you might be thinking, *You think you know the only way forward! Come on, there's only one way? You have to be kidding. There are as many ways to pursue God's dreams in our neighborhoods as there are neighborhoods, probably more.*

This is true to a certain extent. There are ideas, tactics, strategies, ventures, and nearly unlimited collaborations. But if these are pioneered without deep listening, we usually find ourselves in equally deep trouble. Still pushing back? Then think about any hurt, abiding sadness, or even abuse you have suffered from a church community. Dig into it, and at the source is a person or a team who refused to keep listening to the Spirit in context and decided they would force the issue.

They took matters into their own hands and made something happen through their power. More times than not (though not always), they thought they were doing the right thing. We can go all the way back to the ancient Garden story and see that our refusal to listen to the Spirit is the earliest impulse of sin.[5] We think we know better; we think we can make it happen. This is a lie as old as time. But if we prioritize listening as the primary medium of how we can be the church, we can guarantee adventures to tell our grandkids about.

It sounds so simple: learn to pay attention to how the Spirit is working in my life and neighborhood (see fig. 3.1). But the truth is that few of us have been taught to make this our default position. In fact, it might just be the single greatest challenge we have as Christians living in a post-Christian culture. We live and breathe in a culture that has roundly rejected the idea of God's agency in our everyday life. We have moved beyond it as we've moved beyond the horse and carriage. The ideas that God is real—and good—and still active are concepts we have essentially rejected in our everyday life. But as Charles Taylor notes, we are still haunted by the sacred.[6]

Figure 3.1. The Spirit is working in our lives and neighborhoods

Learning to pay attention to God is not a skill we can pick up like we might learn to play guitar, cook Thai food, or take up ballroom dancing. It's the starting and ending place for all Christian formation and the primary path to becoming fully human. If we want to be a healthier, more empathetic, and more grounded people, then we need to become experts in the art of paying attention to the Spirit at work. This critical skill is not just for a renewal of the church or for the healing of the world, but for our own transformation. In order to look back at our lives and be filled with gratitude and awe for the stories we got to be a part of, we need to become lifelong learners of the art of paying attention to the Holy Spirit in our ordinary lives. Even though I've spent much of my life in ministry settings and even earned a master of divinity degree, this critical skill was underdeveloped. I was taught how to communicate the good news of the resurrection and of Christ and his kingdom, but the accent was always on what happened then, not on what God is doing now. If we ignore God's current activity, then it's easy to think we need to fight the battle rather than implement God's victory accomplished by the faithfulness of Christ. Is it really better that Jesus left earth to send "the Helper"? How we answer this question will affect what we believe our responsibility is and what is God's.

How Rob Bell Gave Me a Savior's Complex

When I was growing up, I was taught to believe that Jesus died for my sins so I could go to heaven when I die. The key emphasis was, of course, the cure for death. This is truly good news. But I always kept thinking: *I'm not dead yet, so how am I supposed to live?* Like millions of others I found this angle on the gospel lacking and wondered if I would ever encounter a story big enough that would require my entire life. If the gospel didn't really require anything of my whole life, I wasn't sure I could trust it. I needed a Savior for this life just as much as for the next.

In high school and college I didn't have a name for it, but looking back I would say I was a Christian agnostic. It wasn't that I didn't believe what I was taught—I honestly didn't have much angst about faith—but I had a hard time being around other Christians and definitely didn't want to be in a church service once or twice a week. I was still hunting for a story big enough to give my life to, a gospel that could transform everything. Of course, it didn't come all at once, but in fits and starts through new relationships and experiences something began to change. I began to see that this gospel story was much bigger than I originally thought. Around the year 2003, I think I heard my first Rob Bell tape. It was a talk he gave at Willow Creek Community Church that had to do with goats in Leviticus: not the standard fare for flipping one's world upside down. Of course, I had plenty of other influences at the time, but for a twenty-something idealist from a small town in Wisconsin, Rob Bell's message was a revelation.

I devoured every one of his talks as if it was a never-before-released early recording of my favorite band. He was using the Bible to articulate a bigger *why* than just going to heaven when I die. He showed me that God wants to heal everything, and that, as he put it, "everything is spiritual." I finally found a faith I could give my life to—and herein lies the slippery slope of my savior's complex. I set myself up, and I wonder if the same could be true for others.

Please don't get me wrong, the vision of God seeking to change the world still captures my imagination and has propelled me toward a bright vision and purpose for my life. If we don't orient our lives around a big *why*, we are in trouble from the beginning. But there is a catch, and it's a big one. Over and over again I have fallen into the trap that once I discern God's dreams on an intellectual level, then ipso facto my new job is to make it happen or at least communicate it on bigger and better stages. Here is what I mean. I can easily take this world-changing hope and make it useful. I don't need God to actually be at work in people's lives. I just need a metastory so I can get to work. See the difference?

In one scenario I'm in charge, with a newfound theological energy that leads me to be the savior. When I have the story but don't need God to be active in it, I have way more agency and know that at the end of the day this was my work. In the other scenario I'm dependent on God to act. Frankly, that's just as unnerving as it sounds. I release the burden I was never meant to carry, but it's terrifying to believe that God is actually as good and active as I want to be true. It takes honest-to-goodness trust to believe that the Holy Spirit is working at all, much less in us or all around us or even out ahead of us. Do we have this kind of faith? I'm not talking about a mental assent to a theological proposition here but how we see and how we act in our real lives. It *does* have to do with everywhere we look and is a challenge in every moment.

If there is certainty, if there is no risk, if we are in charge, then we can't call it faith. Once we feel like we have the answer and our job is simply to strategize and implement, we are on a slippery slope toward either pride or shame. And if we don't think God is inviting us into this grand adventure and there is no way we could participate meaningfully in this big story, then we are stuck too. Essentially, we must stay on the narrow path of constantly listening to the Spirit in context. If we try to take over, we get in big trouble. And if we don't think our lives and stories and gifts can be used in God's huge story of redemption, then the adventure ends before it begins. What's more, these cycles of pride and shame are often connected to each other.

When we don't trust that the Spirit is already at work and therefore we need to be the savior, we instantly find ourselves in a figure eight of pride and shame. The disruption of this figure eight is called repentance, recognizing our need for salvation. The task of living both individually and collectively as called away from this spiral of deception could be called active trust. When we stop paying attention to the Spirit at work, we find ourselves with the treacherous and confusing spiral of deception, which is illustrated in figure 3.2.

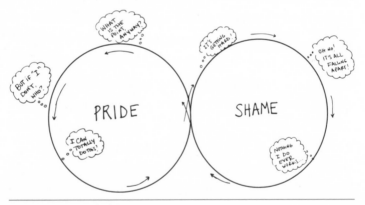

Figure 3.2. The spiral of deception

I know that it's not superfun to talk about sin, but think of it this way: all sin is rooted in the fear of being fully human. We either want to stretch beyond our humanity and try to be like God, or we sink below our humanity and refuse to be human. This is why repentance shouldn't be so scary—it's simply doing a 180-degree turn back toward our identity as beloved human beings. I need salvation from my pride, and I need salvation from my shame. If we're honest, we all do. And when we try to do things together as a community, as a people, as a collective, we need salvation from our collective pride and shame as well. This is to be expected. As we read through Scripture, we notice a pattern of God humbling the proud and lifting up those who are ashamed. Is this mercy or judgment? It feels like the same thing to me. In order to return to what it means to be human, we need both at the same time.

To live without sin is to be fully human, which will be a glorious sight to behold for every one of us. When communities of people learn how to be human together, that glory is multiplied many times over. Ever wonder why Jesus seems pretty obsessed with forgiveness? It stems from his passion that we can rest in being human. This is how we learn to be completely dependent on God. A telltale sign I've noticed within myself in regard to pride is when I feel myself wanting to be helpful more than curious. This is a reality we need to face head-on.

Don't Be Helpful, Be Curious

From a landscape view of much of the church, at least the church in North America, we can make a case that we are just as much communities with a savior's complex as we are communities confessing the need for a Savior. But before we beat ourselves up too much, it might be helpful to take a step back and think about how our inability to pay attention to the Spirit at work has been our default. We have been meticulously trained and rewarded to be helpful rather than curious, and this gets us in trouble.

Most of us were taught that kind and loving people are enthusiastically helpful. I've told my boys that "How can I help?" is one of the most powerful questions they can ever use. I stand by that. But I also need to teach them that honest curiosity needs to precede the very good desire to help. Most people who end up in a ministry setting get there because they want to serve. We are taught servant leadership, which sounds awfully biblical. And besides, it feels good to be helpful. Could there be a downside to being helpful?

When we look more closely at the vast majority of the words of Jesus, they point to our primary task as listening and seeing how God is the active agent before we become active —helpful. While this might sound like a Sunday school slogan, we've seen how it's actually a massive shift from our default posture of being in charge. Pastor and author José Humphreys uses the powerful term "sacred curiosity."[7] Taking this seriously could radically transform our relationship to God, to each other, and to our neighbors.

At a Parish Collective conference my friend Peter Block once said to a group of neighborhood leaders, "Don't be helpful, be curious."[8] I'm not sure if this hits you as a zinger, but for most of my life in church settings the default has been the reverse: Don't be curious, be helpful. In other words, we have the answers, because people are in need of them. Our task is to provide answers. I was not taught that curiosity in almost all relationships (friends, family, neighbors, work) is the beginning of everything truly interesting.

Many books have been written about this, and I'd encourage everyone to dig more into it. But in looking at church history and particularly the history of colonization, many of us, especially from the United States—especially men and white folks like myself—have accepted the idea that progress depends on extending our ideas and achievements toward the people who are classified as needing help.[9]

When we switch from trying to implement God's dream to listening for it as our primary and most critical action, we have done more than shifted a strategy. It might not seem like such a huge deal, but if we, collectively, can go on a journey in which listening for where God is working is our primary endeavor, it flips the script on church as usual. I don't think it's too dramatic to say that if this is *how* we move forward, there are implications for our lives and neighbors and cities that we can barely fathom. It's true that if we don't recover the grounded imagination of the big *why* in our everyday places, there can be no real movement, but if we don't trust that the Spirit is already at work in these places, then any movement we create, even with the best of intentions, has a high probability of collapsing into human effort. Eventually, we will end up tumbling into a knotted ball of pride and shame.

The practice of paying attention to the Spirit is profoundly countercultural. Everywhere we go, most of what we read and the majority of what we watch tells us that we are in charge of our own lives: it's up to us to make them amazing. But if we are after God's dream for our particular places, then we need to remember that God's Spirit is the central character, and we are only supporting actors. Willie James Jennings makes this point at the outset of his magisterial commentary on the book of Acts. He says, "There is only one central character in this story of Acts. It is God, the Holy Spirit. God moves and we respond. We move and God responds."[10]

One of the quickest ways to flip the script of me-centered existence is to look out our front door and realize that God is already active. I wish I could say this has become instinctual for me. I wish I could tell stories of how I have slowly reformed my mind and heart to truly see. I wish every time my feet hit the ground I could remember I'm on sacred, enchanted, holy ground.

The truth is that it takes continual practice and continual remembering, and it is impossible to do alone. To become the kind of church we dream of becoming will mean we make a pact with friends that we will resist the dominant narrative that we are the agents of change. If it's up to us, then it basically boils down to our strategies of implementation.

We will find ourselves in real trouble if we develop a savior's complex—but the reverse is just as dangerous. If we start to think there is no hope or that we are not invited by the Spirit into this grand drama, we are also lost from the beginning. We cannot let pride win the day, but neither can we let shame take us out.

Brené Brown Channeling John the Baptist

Whoever would have thought that a social science researcher on a topic as repulsive as shame would break through to become such a highly sought-after teacher and communicator? If you haven't read anything from Brené Brown or seen her TED talk, you are missing out on a thinker and researcher for such a time as this. She has focused her academic research largely on how shame can dominate the potential of our lives. Through hundreds of stories using the methodology of grounded research, she articulates a message that millions have needed to hear. Besides each of her books being on the *New York Times* bestseller list, she's in the top 1 percent of in-demand speakers in the United States. She's become a pretty big deal.

Why? One reason is that it's difficult to read Brené's work or hear her speak and not feel like she is on your side, fighting for you. But the real reason she is so popular is that she includes herself in the quest to become fully human. She doesn't present herself as having figured it all out. In fact, most of her stories are about messing up and getting up again. Even though she has an academic pedigree and a huge platform, her authority comes from her vulnerability. In my opinion she has become a globally renowned ringleader of repentance. She might not use those words, but this is a significant reason for her success. She has shown how vulnerability means being honest with what is actually going on, and courage is having the gumption to keep figuring out how to be human. On Brené's website bio her message is boiled down to its essence: "I believe that you have to walk through vulnerability to get to courage, therefore . . . embrace the suck."[11] Sounds like the kind of street preacher we need today.

I know some might be thinking, *Yes, that's good, but c'mon. John the Baptist pointed directly to Jesus, and that's not the central message of Brené Brown.* Fair enough, but her primary job is as a social scientist professor and researcher. Our job as faith communities can be to use the insights and gifts she offers and become a community in which our everyday lives embody repentance and point to the need of the Savior. This means that as we pursue God's dream in our particular places, to be human is to be dependent on the Spirit because we don't have it all figured out.

It also means we must cling to the radical idea that without making anything happen we already belong to God, and we already belong to one another.

It means that working out our salvation will be made visible as we connect these two realities in the context of our everyday life. We cannot pursue God's dream of reconciliation and renewal without experiencing it ourselves. We cannot call others to belong to God and one another if we don't rest in this reality ourselves.

There is no conceivable way we can plot our way toward becoming a hopeful force for change if we need to manufacture this reality. It is already true and nothing we do makes it untrue. We can't force it, we can't crank it out, and we can't shoehorn this gift onto others. It needs to be freely received, freely offered, freely trusted.

We already belong to God, and we already belong to one another. Our work is not making it true. In fact, I don't think our work is even primarily telling other people it's true (though I think that's really important). What is most important is living together in such a way that nothing we say, nothing we do, nothing we scheme is a fearful escape. Isn't this an expression of our faith that our neighbors are hoping to see? If this is true, we are definitely going to need each other.

This Magic Is for Everyone

Not everyone can keep the attention of a room of five hundred people for forty minutes. Not everyone can sing passionately in front of others. Not everyone can manage a complex organization. But we all can pay attention. Paying attention is magical because it's not just for the talented few. It's open to all of us. If we are honest, it's required of us. The truth is that we are always paying attention to something, and in this sense we can't not pay attention. The task is to train our attention on God's activity, and the rest will fall into place. Another way of saying this is "seek first the kingdom of God and everything else will be added to you" (Matthew 6:33 paraphrased). Another way to paraphrase this command from Jesus might be, "Listen, and join what I am doing in your neighborhood, and don't worry about the results."

Paying attention to what God is doing all over the place and still having the capacity to enter into it is overwhelming. While we have been discussing the art of paying attention, we haven't focused on *where* we need to focus our attention. In order to do this with others, we need a literal common ground.

I trust that you are an amazing human being, but on your own, you can never be the church. It requires a team of listeners. Unless we have a focused place to listen, we cannot have a focused place to discern and act on what the Spirit is doing in that place. This turns out to be good news.

CHAPTER FOUR

THE MEGACHURCH
NEXT DOOR

You are Christ's body—that's who you are!
You must never forget this.

APOSTLE PAUL, *THE MESSAGE*

'm about to say something that almost no self-respecting
person would say out loud: I wanted to be a rock-star pastor.

It might not come as a huge surprise given what I told
you about my theological journey and how my savior's complex
requires salvation. But keep in mind I'm not saying it in the
confidential confines of a therapist's office or an accountability
group. I'm putting this on paper in a published book, which
means I'll have to live with this confession until the paper
decomposes. I'm trying to help you understand what's at risk:
I mean, my kids will grow up with this information. Once
someone knows this, they can't unknow it. I want people to like
me, and I don't think this will help.

It's still embarrassing to admit, but I think it's an appropriate place to begin, because just ten years ago this was a pretty

51

common aspiration for most of my male peers in seminary. (See how I'm already starting to blame others?) Just to be clear, it wasn't so much the "preaching in an expensive leather jacket and hanging out with celebrities" vibe I was going for. But it was spending twenty-five hours a week (or more) working on a sermon and building just about all the components of the church around the preaching and Sunday morning experience. It was being able to keep the rapt attention of hundreds and ideally thousands of people. It was being increasingly in demand. It was essentially betting the organizational culture and vision of a church on what I hoped would be amazing sermons. I know this might sound a little odd now, but I was not the only one thinking this way. For plenty of people discerning a vocational call to ministry, the wave of the seeker-sensitive movement had picked up momentum and was finding new energy among Gen-X pastors. At least it felt that way to me.

Ten or fifteen years ago some interesting theological movements were growing around the mission of God, around embracing doubt, and especially around cultivating a Sunday experience in which our friends who wouldn't call themselves Christians were made to feel welcome. That part was most attractive to me. Maybe there was a way for us as a church to set a warm, hospitable table not for ourselves but for others. Perhaps you've heard the quote: "The church is the only organization on earth that exists for its nonmembers."[1] I wanted to see this happen, and I was willing to give my life for it.

But one day everything was flipped around. In fact, it was the day I met Paul Sparks, who has become one of my dearest friends and the cofounder of the Parish Collective. Paul was hosting a gathering for pastors and church planters at their cool warehouse music venue in downtown Tacoma. I guess it's ironic that my dream of being a rock-star pastor was deconstructed in a music venue where a church met on Sundays. Paul had invited two relatively unknown Australian missiologists, Alan Hirsch and Michael Frost, to a special invite-only event I was fortunate enough to attend. It was quite a day. I remember Mark Driscoll and his posse of pastors leaving in a huff at the lunch break after disagreeing with Michael on the importance of preaching. This foreshadowed the internal drama within me that would play out in the afternoon.

Those who have heard Michael Frost speak know he's an exceptionally talented communicator. He has a mesmerizing way of waving his hands, telling a story, and landing a fresh idea. To be blunt, he has the gifts and qualities needed to build a megachurch. While I was listening to him speak, I was already plotting how I could get more recordings of his talks. So that afternoon, when he told us all that he had committed to not speak for the first couple years of their young church plant, I nearly fell off my chair.

He went on to explain that while he might possess some of the gifts to attract Christians from all over the broader Sydney region, he and the team were making an explicit decision to avoid building the church around this gift. I found this idea as scandalous as it was profound. This is like having LeBron James on your basketball team and keeping him on the bench. It's just not something people do unless they're trying to play a different game—which is exactly what was going on. The team decided that Michael's rhetorical gifts were perfectly suited to building a community on the flawless execution of the pinnacle of the religious consumer experience, the home-run sermon. But they wanted to play a different game. They were trying to figure out how to be a community in a particular place. They were trying to orient their lives around a set of shared practices. They weren't trying to attract Christians to their brilliant show; they were trying to figure out what it means to be the church in their everyday life. This simple reversal transformed my imagination in a single moment. Of course, these ideas had been building for some time, but to hear of such a drastic move made me feel like the ground had shifted beneath my feet.

Now, it feels sort of obvious.

While this story is revealing, I bet you can see why I find it a little embarrassing. I was embedded in a framework of white evangelicalism in which most of the leadership is male and charismatic, which is exactly what I was aiming toward. This isn't so much of an apology as it is an important acknowledgment that this story comes from a particular culture and social location. There are many beautiful expressions of the church not nearly as centered on the charisma and talent of the preacher. Nevertheless, whether we tend to orient our churches on the skills of the preacher, the execution of the programs, or any of the cool offerings of the church itself, it's a telltale sign that we are flipping the *what* of our church programs with the *why* of God's dream in our context (see fig. 4.1).

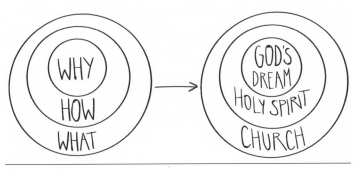

Figure 4.1. The proper view

With the framework I have borrowed from Simon Sinek, it's time I talk about the final circle in its proper place: the *what*. This was the original light-bulb moment for me because I was essentially taught that the church itself belonged in the middle: that the church is the *why*. I had heard phrases like "the church is the hope of the world" and it's an "unstoppable force" so often that I began to believe the point of the church is a larger church. So many of us have been inspired by the potential and promise of a healthy local church, and the last thing I want to do is pour water on that fire. I believe we need the local church more than ever. I'm still giving my life to this vision. But there has to be a way to be the church in our everyday lives that doesn't demand the center of our collective life together hinging on the production quality of our gatherings. It is nearly impossible to frame the organizing life of the church around the Sunday experience and not compare ourselves with other Sunday experiences. When we mistakenly turn the church itself into the big *why*, we get caught up in a competition to see who can get more people. It's like we have inadvertently found ourselves competing for market share in the consumer category of religion. This default mode, which so many of us have bought into, slowly transforms our view of the church into a weekly teaching and singing event for religious consumers.

In this generation we need to make a choice. We must choose between the long road of faithful presence in a place that demonstrates and invites people to become apprentices of Jesus or to keep pushing the weekly hype machine built on spiritualized self-help and emotionally charged music focused on the individual and their personal preferences.

I see the choice like this:

Historic Experience of What the Church Is
+ a community of people
+ joining in God's dreams
+ in a particular place
+ with their everyday lives

Current Experience of What the Church Is
+ individual consumers together
+ pursuing the American Dream
+ wherever it suits them
+ reinforced by a local Sunday event or online

I know I'm pushing this last definition as far as it will go, but honestly I don't think it's that much of a stretch. The great Marshall McLuhan famously said "the medium is the message,"[2] and when we equate the church with the event, the message is that we are consumers. This is perhaps the single greatest reason we are on the precipice of a meltdown. In my opinion this is why people are leaving the church in droves. If the church is just another optional consumer choice, it's just too small of a story to give our lives to. There has to be something more.

I believe this is the primary reason why millennials, who have uniquely been shaped to sniff out agendas and inauthenticity, are saying no thank you to the church. It isn't that it's not cool enough or tech savvy enough, but that we don't need another product. We need an integrative vision that points to how we can live together. We need a vision that addresses the unraveling of society and the injustices we see playing out all around us. We need a story that everyone can belong to, a story we can receive as a gift as opposed to earning the American Dream. We need a story that refuses to see some people as poor or less than regardless of what's in their bank account or the color of their skin. We are literally dying for a story that can be good news in our everyday lives. Enough with the entertainment! The future is calling people who will believe another way is possible. Our continued language and culture related to the church as a product needs to be called out. We need to say no. We need to stop saying that we can call this second definition a church, because it's not.

If we can't find our way out of this smaller story in which the church itself is the big *why*, we will almost assuredly stay within this never-ending vortex (see fig. 4.2).

Remember how my wife and I are training

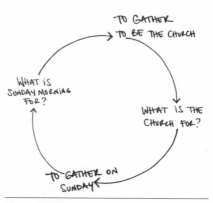

Figure 4.2. The never-ending vortex

(manipulating?) our son to never say "going to church"? Well, this is a big reason why. I don't want him buying into the false narrative swirling and spinning all around him. By the way, if you want to join me in this rhetorical campaign with your beloved children or grandchildren, and they ask if you are going to church, you can smile and say, "Oh honey, going to church is ontologically impossible." I promise it's fun to say this, and it's important if we want to stop the madness.

They Come Every Year

I'll never forget hearing about the annual church-plant migration story from my friend Mark Scandrette. Mark and Lisa and their kids have been living in the Mission District of San Francisco since 1999. Few neighborhoods have changed as dramatically in twenty years. It has been transformed into a hipster mecca. But that's definitely not what it was like when Mark and Lisa first moved in. Over time they have emerged as elders in the area and are often called on to connect new people and help to explain the unique cultural makeup of San Francisco. As such, a good percentage of church planters find their way to Mark, who has held countless meetings with church-plant teams who have just moved to San Francisco.

He told me he has been around long enough to see the following pattern repeat itself every year. Annually, three or four well-funded church-plant teams move to San Francisco. Sometimes a team consists of just a couple; sometimes a few families move there to become the initial team. Since San Francisco is seen as so liberal and post-Christian, it's been deemed one of the most difficult places in the United States to start a new faith community. There is sort of an "if you can make it there, you can make it anywhere" mentality to church planting. This cultural narrative goes a long way toward fundraising in many Christian cultures. Each year roughly four teams venture out from the South or the Midwest with hopes of starting a new faith community.

A well-funded church plant is expected to have at least one to two hundred people attending their church after a year or two. If this doesn't happen, they can't keep going. Essentially, the question that's always on their mind is, How do we get more people to our gathering? If we can do that, we can make it. And if we can't get this many people, the game is over. This is the metric that drives everything.

If they can hit this tipping point, they are off and running. So, what usually happens? Among the four church plants, one is able to "make it" within the first year. They become the hot new thing in town, and the buzz helps them gather seventy-five to one hundred visitors a week. And they are off and running. Most of the people come from other churches or perhaps have recently graduated from a Christian college. The other three struggle and usually end up feeling like failures. They often go home with a profound sense of loss and sincere questions about their vocation and identity. They wrestle with whether or not they truly heard from God. This was not a small endeavor. They bet everything on this venture. Marriages are often compromised, kids are moved, and an enormous amount of money is spent. After all of this extraordinary sacrifice, they either need to go home or quickly find a job because the bills are stacking up.

Here's the thing, while the church that makes it still has momentum, the following September, just as school is starting again, they realize they are now a sophomore, and four new freshmen are coming up. Within a few years they are no longer the cool new thing and get displaced by the winner of the incoming class. This cycle repeats year after year and creates the illusion that if you build it, they will come. This cycle is perpetuated in dozens of cities every year. For some reason we keep elevating this "small" story of church growth, and it's killing us. We need to shift our imaginations toward the much larger story of what God is doing and how we join in.

Hillsong Is Tiny

You might be thinking, *Yeah, but what about the rise of mega-churches? What about, for example, the global network of Hillsong Churches that are thriving all over the world, especially in places that are seen as post-Christian?* Great point! Spanning the globe, Hillsong has grown into its own denomination. With sites from snowy Kiev to sunny Bali, over 130,000 people are connected to Hillsong. It's pretty incredible and certainly demands our attention.

But we should also put it into perspective. According to the Pew Research Center, there are 2.18 billion Christians in the world. If my math is correct, that makes people connected to Hillsong 0.02 percent of the Christians in the world. And here is where it gets much more interesting.

Let's say that right now in your neighborhood there are ten thousand people. If you take the Pew Research claim that 33 percent of the world consider themselves Christians, with the United States having the largest number, then potentially that would mean there are at least 3,300 people in your neighborhood who consider themselves Christians.

That is a megachurch.

Even if we say only 10 percent of these people are really interesting in following Jesus and joining in God's dreams for their neighborhood, that's a vibrant, healthy, and substantial community of 330 people! Not bad. The odds are high that there is a ridiculous abundance of people, resources, ideas, and brilliance all around us. This is almost assuredly true right where you live, right now. It's just that we have no way to organize ourselves; we have no way to connect even though we live in the most digitally connected culture of all time.

If we change the game to joining in God's dream in our neighborhood, and if all of us listen and discern the Spirit in our everyday lives, then what are we left with? The truth is that there is a hidden, disconnected megachurch in all of our neighborhoods. There's a dizzying amount of abundance hidden in plain sight. We just don't have the capacity to see because we have focused on something else. Without a doubt, the fastest way to see church growth happen is to shift our point of view. If we have the eyes to see and can make the right connections, the potential of a thriving local church is everywhere we look.

Right Here, Right Now

In her beautifully written memoir on learning to see God at work all around her, Shannan Martin writes that "attentiveness is prayer breathed at the street level."[3] I absolutely love this idea, but I also wonder how God might be attentive to us on our streets, longing for us to fit together as the church.

Think about this. Christians—one of the largest people groups in the world—are effectively invisible to one another. If the followers of Jesus were connected globally, we would be far larger than most nations. We would likely have assets in the trillions of dollars. We would find representation in every stratum of culture and instantly be connected around the world. It is astonishing that people like us, who are disconnected and hidden in plain sight, likely make up the largest voluntary association in the world. Companies like Facebook have become enormously profitable and powerful by making connections visible. It makes me wonder what would happen if we could make our connections visible as we become the church in our everyday lives.

I believe it would make Facebook look pathetic. Each of us steward the astonishing story of the resurrection as an exclamation point on God's salvation. But, on our own, we remain effectively invisible. If we can't be connected in our everyday lives, then we won't be visible to our actual neighbors. Missiologist Lesslie Newbigin says quite directly that the church "is a visible community among other human communities." We are called to be a public and visible community among other public and visible communities, and this is no small matter. Newbigin goes on to say, "The whole core of biblical history is the story of a visible community to be God's own people, His royal priesthood on earth, the bearer of His light to the nations." And finally to drive the point home, Newbigin says, "It is surely a fact of inexhaustible significance that what our Lord left behind Him was not a book, nor a creed, nor a system of thought, nor a rule of life, but a visible community."[4] As a way of imagining what is possible, let me invite you into a somewhat dangerous mental exercise.

For just a second try to imagine yourself as God. (Did I just invite you into idolatry? My apologies if that freaks you out.) What I mean is pretend you have the perspective of God and you are lovingly viewing all of your creation. Among all the pain and violence and beauty and joy, you know that billions of your beloved already want to follow Jesus and love their neighbors. The primary obstacle is that they don't know one another. Even more painful is that the vision of these people fitting together as a team is subverted by the idea that the church exists for itself.

If God's dream is for the church to function as a body, each part working together for the flourishing of each place and connecting across each place, then we have a vision to belong to. If we see the church as splintered institutions competing for the market share of attention once a week, that's exactly what we end up with. We get to choose, but we should use our Bibles and intellect and the shared desires of our hearts in discerning the purpose of the church. This is no small matter. This is not primarily a question about religious affiliation, about choosing a team to cheer for as we do in sports. This is about naming the story we choose to orient our collective lives around. How we frame and understand what the church is *for* will dramatically alter how we understand the economy and politics and, well, literally everything else. That is, at least if we dare to believe that God is at work renewing and restoring everything. We will be in far better shape if we dare to believe this to be true and acknowledge we have no idea how to actually get there than if we give up on this vision from the beginning. But we *can* get after it. The first step ahead of us is simply having the courage to embrace the extraordinary gift that is our own limitations.

The Gift of Limits

When we stretch our arms as high as they will go, unless we have Inspector Gadget-like powers, they will reach a point we cannot reach beyond. This reality is a remarkable gift. We have a body and are a body, which means we are creatures. As a beautiful creation we were made with limits, and if we seek to ignore or transcend these limits, we get into trouble. This is true of our energy, our time, our attention, and our capacity. Just as this is true for us individually with our bodies, it's true for us collectively as a local church. If we don't learn how to embrace our limits, it's nearly impossible for us to ask any of the questions we have been asking so far.

It might feel sort of obvious at this point, but if we dare to ask about God's dream, and we believe our path will depend and rely on the Spirit, and if we need to do this together as a team, then we will absolutely need common ground for any of this to come together as a way of life. This is where the contrast between the church as a Sunday event and becoming the church in our everyday life gets real. The hopes and ideas and longings of our very particular places are where these questions about what God is up to take on literal shape.

Most of us have been taught that we need to apply the universal truths of God to our particular lives. While I believe this is true in theory, if this is the standard experience of what it means to be the church, then I'm afraid we've got it backward. We are limited, finite, created people, and that's how we experience the world. We are not God. We do not have universal wisdom and knowledge. Everything we experience *comes from particularity*. Each of us is unique: our neighborhood is unique, our story is unique, and all of these truths are what make us individually interesting. If we want to climb the ladder, if we want to dominate, if we want to get others to be like us, then by all means we should accentuate the universal. But if we want to be human, if we want to invite others into a truly human story, then we need to honor the particular. Of course, there are best practices, there is wisdom that can connect across space and time, but like any relationship, if we don't honor and work with what is literally right in front of us, we aren't being faithful.

Imagine that I tell my wife she can rest easy because I have mastered the seven laws of marriage and all I have to do is apply them to her and we will always be happy. She will either laugh in my face or get angry. When we skip over the complex realities of our own stories and our own places because we have a universal agenda to implement, we usually wind up in trouble. As created ones, this is neither how we experience the world nor how we like to be treated. There is no one else like us, there is no one else who has our particular story, and there is no place we should treat exactly the same. If we are going to join in God's universal dream of shalom, there is only one way we can actually approach it—from the particular. We can't join the Spirit in the abstraction of everywhere, but if we and a few friends do so in the particular of our actual lives, then with this switch of perspective we could see a growing movement.

The implications of this are jaw dropping and set the table for a new way to think about the actual places where we live, and it's to this possibility we must turn next.

CHAPTER FIVE

THE PARISH IS
THE UNIT OF CHANGE

*Culture changes when a small group of people,
often on the margins of society, find a better way to live,
and other people begin to copy them.*

DAVID BROOKS

H ave you ever read the headline of an article that someone posted on social media and immediately shared the article before you even read it? I know this is a horrible practice, but when I saw David Brooks's column in the *New York Times* titled "The Neighborhood Is the Unit of Change," I was so overjoyed to see these seven words strung together that I sent it everywhere I could before even reading the piece. A guilty feeling soon rushed over me as I realized I had become what I hate about social media. Thankfully, I was relieved as I quickly read it and found myself cheering each passing sentence like I was cheering for my beloved Chicago Cubs in the bottom of the ninth inning. I found myself shouting "yes, yes, yes" out loud, leaving my chocolate lab, Theo, rather perplexed.

The essence of the article is that as a culture, we have bet on a theory of change based on helping one person at a time. This gamble is not working. We need to transform our imagination. Helping one person at a time is a lot better than not helping at all, but if we want holistic change, as Brooks states, "you have to think about changing many elements of a single neighborhood, in a systematic way, at a steady pace."[1] The neighborhood represents a subversive alternative to how we imagine change happens. We don't need to choose between focusing all of our attention on a charity model centered on individuals or a bureaucratic model centered on systems. There is a third way. At the neighborhood level we can simultaneously champion individual heroes and work hard to create just and equitable systems.

This crucial third way is located in our neighborhoods, but for our purposes as followers of Jesus, I will advocate for the better word *parish*. In the book *The New Parish*, we define this ancient word with some fresh language that has served us well. For our purposes let's define the *parish* as a "geographic area that's large enough to live life together (live, work, play, etc.) and small enough to be known as a character within it."[2] In an urban context this generally equates to a neighborhood, in more suburban areas it might be the entire suburb, and in rural areas it might encompass a much larger geographic area with some common centers like a few pubs, the granary, or local schools. Getting clear about the particularity of our parish is important if we hope to avoid the seesaw effect of prioritizing only individuals to the neglect of systems and vice versa.

It's been my experience that more conservative Christians focus more on the morality of individuals while progressives highlight injustices at the systemic level. Both are absolutely critical. But if we don't have a small enough environment to witness the cause-and-effect relationship between individuals and systems, we always revert back to our initial impulse. This is why the parish is such a profound place to begin. In today's polarized culture, the parish is an invitation to reality for all of us. At the everyday level in the parish, we get to see and feel and learn from the effects of our actions. We can't do that when our efforts are focused on the whole city.

If we hope to engage in God's healing dream, we need an approach that simultaneously honors individual people, the systems we have created, and the dynamic relationship in which people influence systems and systems influence people. By naming the parish as the unit of change, we reclaim the parish as the literal ground where our practiced faith becomes a powerful and even subversive organizing platform. The parish gives shape and definition to our imagination as we dream about real people and places and their very real stories.

In order to practice our faith together, we need an area large enough to live (e.g., the potential to live, work, and play) and small enough for us to be known as a character in the story of that place.[3] If we dare to imagine what God's dreams might be, and we want to follow the Spirit, then we need a shared geography to move us from an abstract idea to a very real dare. The parish is the playground where God can invite us into practical hope. If our longings are submitted to God's desires in our parish, we won't succumb to some obscure, abstract theological argument. Instead, we will receive a gift unique to us, a particular vision that dares us to take action. This is so dramatically different from going to the latest conference, bringing home a binder full of ideas, and implementing a strategy. This is not a faddish new program. Once we have a place of practice, it will become the context of our own formation even as we seek to join in its transformation.

As the body is to a person, the parish is to the team. It gives us common ground, a limited place of responsibility, and a space that allows us to participate and even lead within the multiple systems that shape our common life. Isn't this what we need today? We don't need more formulas and techniques to crank out new plans. We need a place to listen and learn. We need a place where we can feel the effects of our actions and make creative iterations. We need a place where we can pursue the dreams of God within our common life. More than we need God to convince others of some abstract idea, we need God to show up for us in our actual lives because we are incapable of living out these dreams on our own. There is a significant difference between our need for God's activity and presence and simply using God for our purposes.

Scholars have long emphasized the profound difference between the Tower of Babel story in Genesis and the Pentecost story in Acts, between the homogenous empire building of Babel and listening to the Spirit in Acts.[4] A primary difference in these stories hinges on people making things happen through their creative techniques versus a community waiting and listening for God. We would be wise to consider the notion that the Spirit of God is deconstructing and obstructing our contemporary tower-building plans. We might say we created the hot mess of today's church. That would be true. But we can also read a story line of mercy. If we look more carefully, we just might see the mercy of God, who doesn't want our techniques and strategies to win the day.

We serve a God who is jealous for our attention—not because of some divine insecurity complex but because he longs for our freedom and joy. We want techniques because we want control. We want control because we are scared (at least that's usually at the root of my feeble attempts at control). But we serve a God who mercifully obliterates our illusions of control. When we engage the complex life of our parish, we will realize we are not in control. Rather than seeing all the beauty and brokenness of our parish as a project to be completed, we should view it as an epic journey. Once we become characters in the story of our parish, it's difficult to imagine that we could control anything. Then another truth emerges: we need all sorts of companions in this journey.

You Can't Go Alone

This will sound a bit ridiculous, but we can't be the church by ourselves. We cannot take this journey into the parish alone. No one would ever make an argument that we can, but the truth is that the vast majority of the stories we tell, the resources we use, and the songs we sing are about us as individuals. We love to celebrate the solitary hero and to read self-help books. Digital technology is shaping us into the most individualistic culture in the history of humankind. The story line that undergirds so much of our culture is "you can make it happen by yourself if you try harder." But this is tearing our social fabric. David Brooks notes, "Our society suffers from a crisis of connection, a crisis of solidarity. We live in a culture of hyper-individualism."[5] Our task is to build a community with the vision and capacity to create local culture.

For far too long, Christians have employed endless strategies to get more people to come to our church programs. Against the tide of decline, we revert to the default: try to make our programs and services more attractive. Meanwhile the long game—which is the only game that matters—is profoundly neglected. The long game cultivates, nurtures, and creates vibrant local cultures. If we cease to do this, it's nearly impossible to live into the vision put forth by words of Jesus: "You're here to be light, bringing out the God-colors in the world. God is not a secret to be kept" (Matthew 5:15 *The Message*).

Naming this reality as I have is not a quick fix. To get where we are today, we have unintentionally focused on the wrong goal, and it will likely take decades to reimagine and recreate the church. We don't need to be in an anxious rush. But neither can we keep propping up our insecure strategies that place the numerical growth of church attendance above joining God to create a local culture in our parishes.

Culture Eats Strategy for Breakfast

Thousands of pages have been written on the somewhat elusive term *culture*. Let's begin by defining culture as the most important stories we tell ourselves about how we should live. There is no culture-free zone; culture is the water we swim in. But that doesn't mean we can't proactively transform and create new culture. I love Andy Crouch's idea that the "only way to change culture is to make more of it."[6]

Particularly on a local neighborhood level, this is our collective responsibility *and* opportunity. When we build a way of life that others can join as a visible community, we slowly create a new culture. If we don't, the default stories in our neighborhoods will win the day. This means the primary task of the truly local church is to build a local culture that others can experience and step into. We need a focused story (God making everything whole again right here), and there needs to be an invitation (to a way of life right here). This is where evangelism meets discipleship and builds a community. This is the alternative story of the gospel we are meant to integrate into our everyday lives.

To build local culture and embody an alternative story, we need a team. Neither evangelism nor discipleship makes much sense unless we can craft a public way of life together that becomes a plausibility structure that claims the gospel is true. Or perhaps even more important, the gospel is true *here*. The gospel is true *now*. There is good news to be proclaimed in this *place*. Injustices break our hearts right in front of us. Marriages are on the brink of collapse just down the street. Two streets over, kids wonder if they will ever be lovable. Feel the difference? This is not a game. Real lives, relationships, systems, and structures are at stake.

When our reasons for lament and celebration become particular, it's a sign we are getting closer to the heart of God. God doesn't merely love the cosmos. God loves *individuals*, right now, in this particular moment. This is not a Hallmark card platitude. That intimate story of injustice that sparked a fire in you—God loves that reaction in you. That way you feel when you introduce two people who need to know each other—God loves that this makes you so happy. That moment early in the morning when you take your first sip of coffee in your quiet home and you rest in gratitude—God loves that you love to do this. We serve a God of both the universal and the particular, but our experience of God's love and hope for us will always be found in the particularity of our everyday lives. It stands to reason that if the love of God we experience in Christ will always be felt in the particular, then our experience of becoming Christ's body (the church) must as well. It's fun to think about the expansive, universal, even cosmic implications of Christ, but the real action and the real potential is in the particular.

This brings us back to the grounding centrality of why we need actual common ground. If we dare to create local culture, we will need a place to begin, and we will need a team. It can't just be *me* and *my* beautiful intentions.

Better Together

We can't embody this gospel story on our own because we can't belong to ourselves. At least, we cannot belong to ourselves before it gets real weird, real fast. Let me state the obvious: a random network of well-meaning Christians is not a church. The gospel is not merely an invitation to mission or even spiritual formation—it's also an invitation to belonging. If there is no team, there is no possibility of belonging. And if our belonging is primarily built on attending services and programs, we need to concede that 85 percent of our neighbors will opt out before we get started.

The only way local culture can be created is when the story that undergirds our common life (God's dream in our parish) is connected to a sense of belonging. Name any successful movement that changed culture (e.g., the civil rights movement), and we'll likely see not only an alternative story being lived out but an invitation to belong to this new story. If there is no collective embodiment, no belonging, there is no capacity for this story to be lived out by more and more people. John McKnight says, "Being a 'neighbor' is not about living in a particular place; it's about belonging to neighbors who are building a culture of care for each other."[7] We need this truth in order to learn how to be the church in everyday life. We need to discern how to identify and connect other followers of Jesus in order to learn how to be a team.

This is where it might start to feel hard. Some might be thinking, *Are you saying that at some point I need to find a small team that can use our individual gifts and strengths as we keep discerning God's dream and how we join in the Spirit's work?*

That is what I'm saying.

This team might worship with different churches, some might have written off church gatherings a long time ago, and some might be brand new to the faith, but I'm praying that you are open to the process of joining, praying for, or even convening a team. The vast majority of the time there already is a small group, missional community, or established congregation that is deeply involved in the life of the parish. Remember that my wife and I have taught our son to never talk about "going to church"? We have taught him a working definition that he can proudly narrate to just about anyone who asks. He says the church is "Christians in the neighborhood who are joining in God's dreams for that place." This is what I want for you and me. It will require prayer, patience, and refusal to either opt out or give in to the status quo.

If we refuse to do this, then we should be honest about our capitulation to some other set of stories. We can humble ourselves and make ourselves dependent on the living God to show us the way forward, or we can allow the other big stories competing for our attention to guide our way. These other stories are not necessarily bad. We can be proud of our country, but if we buy into the story that our citizenship in a nation trumps our allegiance to the kingdom of God, then we've bought into a culture-building project that's clearly in defiance of Scripture. We can be passionate about justice and human rights, but if the primary story we build our lives on is the law and equity, then we should be prepared to live with a constant spirit of judgment. We have the freedom to pick our most hopeful and expansive stories, but right after we do, they begin to shape us profoundly. When Jesus says, "Seek first the kingdom and all else will be added to you," he's saying that we have to pick our story. This is the question we face each day: What story do we give our utmost allegiance to?

When we become a team that is discerning God's dreams, when we have the courage to follow the Spirit into the particularity of our parishes, we are building a local culture. Our primary task is to build a team that can create a local culture and invite others along. The following paragraphs are some practical steps toward this end.

It's also time for the second set of diagrams of this journey. The first series of circles, patterned after Simon Sinek, is designed to disrupt, reimagine, and reawaken our collective opportunity to the fact that there is another way to be the church in our everyday life. The next series is meant to function more as a practical invitation. While they are ordered this way on purpose because of their implications, you'll see they are not firmly sequential. At the end of the day, if there is not a committed, culture-creating core team, then praying for one will remain a fervent prayer. But if you don't have three or four friends to begin, you can definitely get started in the rings that are farther out. This will make more sense as we journey ahead.

Creating a Minimum Viable Presence

Perhaps the most important task of a team that's seeking to become an expression of the church in the neighborhood is to discern, at both the individual and collective levels, a set of practices to be crafted and adapted. There have been numerous helpful ideas for how people in community can think about what their common life might look like together. It's likely there are as many ways to do this as there are people and places, but I suggest three movements that can prompt this way of life in multiple life-giving directions.[8]

Common mission. As individuals and as a team, what are some commitments we could make to tangibly join God in what God is doing in the neighborhood?

Figure 5.1. The core team

This might be a new venture, serving on a local council, committing to prayer walking each week, or hosting a soup night for the neighborhood. There is no limit here. But the general question is how are we going to roll up our sleeves to take action? This leads us to ask:

✦ What is an individual experiment of presence you can commit to?

✦ What is something already happening in your parish you could all help to cultivate?

✦ What organizations and associations can you strengthen through your collective presence?

Common formation. The question of mission is, What are we to do? And the question of formation asks, Who are we to become? What are the practices that form us into the image of Christ in ways that are unique to us and to our neighborhood? This question is critical not only because we are human *beings* and not human *doings,* but because if mission is the only question, we can easily forget that God does not want us to be mere agents of transformation but to be transformed as well. The practices that help us get there are every bit as vital as the questions of mission. The following are some questions related to common formation:

✦ How do you hope to transform and grow in this season?

✦ What practices of formation will be required to sustain and challenge your own character?

✦ How will you cultivate shared discernment for how you need to grow as a team?

Common relationship. Staying together as a team will take careful and attentive practices. Even as we are engaged in common mission together, in common formation, we need to finally ask how we are cultivating more and more trust.

✦ What are the daily, weekly, and monthly rhythms of connection that are most vital in this season?

✦ Do we need different sizes of groups to accommodate different hopes and capacity for depth?

✦ What are the best environments we need to create to celebrate, lament, and plot the next steps?

Commit Together, Then Do It Again

This first ring of a team hoping to embody the alternative story of the gospel will include the highest level of commitment. The monastic tradition has compelling vows of stability for one's entire life. While there is immense wisdom there, I believe we should start with experiments and experiences through which a small team can grow in trust as they seek to create local culture for at least a year. This way we keep one another accountable and can create space for change and iteration, especially when life throws us curveballs. Dan White Jr. has helpfully suggested using the summer to provide time to reflect and discern adaptations and to create a viable outlet for people who feel they might need to leave the team.[9]

But what about a gathering and liturgy? Without drawing back, without reframing our attention and desires around the centrality of Christ, we will likely find ourselves organizing around a different story. I believe gatherings are critical and liturgy is profoundly important. It's also true that, as Anglican priest Tish Warren says, "God is forming us into a new people, and the place of that formation is in the small moments of today."[10]

If our Sunday liturgies, regardless of tradition, are not forming us to join in pursuing (1) God's kingdom on earth (in our everyday lives), (2) as it is in heaven (God's desire), and (3) as a body or a team that is a visible community, then what is it forming us to be? We need to wrestle with that based on our particular traditions and contexts. If it's true that our

Sunday practices are making it more possible to be a team that is pursuing God's dreams, then we need to keep doing them. If they are not, then perhaps we need to prayerfully lean back into the tradition to unearth the gifts and practices we need for today's new challenges and opportunities.

There Must Be Invitations to Try on This Way of Life

Forming a team is vital to inviting others in. Without a team, the challenges of both evangelism and discipleship are nearly impossible. If we can do this, we can begin to create local culture and invite others into this joyous endeavor. But while this team should think of itself as an expression of the church or even a congregation, a major part of its task is to knit together the local church. The broader mission is to re-member the body of Christ. I'm convinced it will take all sorts of expressions of the church in the context of a parish to begin to see the beauty and power of the church in the neighborhood.

CHAPTER SIX

THE SAME TEAM

The divisions of the Church are a public denial
of the sufficiency of the atonement.

LESSLIE NEWBIGIN

A sh Wednesday is the most underrated day of the Christian year. The practice of marking one's forehead with ashes goes back to the eleventh century.[1] I've learned to look forward to it as I do Christmas. Yes, it's true that it's a day when we remember that we are created from dust and to dust we will return. Yes, it's supposed to be about humility and repentance. So I agree that Ash Wednesday is supposed to be a somber day of reflection and preparation for the liturgical season of Lent. I'm sure this is normal, but it feels a lot more like preparing for Pentecost to me. Let me explain.

I live in the great city of Seattle. It's sometimes portrayed as a post-Christian culture. Studies suggest that the fastest growing religious demographic is the "nones"—people with no religious affiliation. Unlike some other parts of the United States, if someone is hoping to score bonus points in Seattle for saying they're a Christian, they are in the wrong place. While outright scorn is unlikely, it's best to be prepared for annoyed indifference. So smearing our foreheads with a sign of Christian affiliation and the reality of death feels rather countercultural. It's an unusual way to stick out.

Imagine how interesting it is to go downtown or walk around in my neighborhood on this first day of Lent. On that evening I can walk all over town and see all sorts of people with a black cross smudged across their foreheads. They are everywhere! Each year it hits me with more joy and holy discontent. It's the one day of the year when the invisible church becomes much more visible. Across various denominations and traditions, all sorts of women and men obviously are committed to following Jesus. On this one evening each year, I can make out just how much larger the Christian population actually is in comparison to what I imagine. It always lights a fire within me to try to knit more people together. We are all on the same team—we just rarely get to see it.

In May 2019, I was fortunate enough to spend some time in Tangier, Morocco. It was during Ramadan in a city that is about 70 percent Muslim. It was my first time in a predominantly Muslim country. On the first night I recall waking up at midnight and again at 3 a.m. to prayers recited through an amplified speaker for all to hear. In this context there is no question about what it means to practice one's faith in public. There is no hiding behind personal piety and thousands of different denominations; it's woven deeply into the cultural fabric.

I'm not trying to make the case for public prayer, but I do yearn for pathways that allow the invisible Christian community to become more visible. To reflect on how this might be possible, it's helpful to take a few steps back in church history and reflect on how we got to this place of being nearly invisible to neighbors and one another.

The Reformer and the Marriage Therapist

Martin Luther famously nailed his Ninety-Five Theses to the church door in Wittenberg, Germany, drawing a well-defined line in the sand that is credited with igniting the Protestant Reformation. But Luther's act was a testament to fidelity and betrayal at the same time. Most scholars would agree Luther was not attempting to forge an alternative to the Roman Catholic Church. He did not hope to break away and start something new, but to reshape something very old. It would have been inconceivable to think that those ninety-five theses would result in the creation of Lutheranism, which today includes 74.2 million people around the world, much less the entire Protestant arm of the church. Whoever could have guessed that for every one of the ninety-five theses posted, an average of 474 denominations would be created by the twenty-first century? That's right: according to some counts there are well over forty-five thousand denominations.[2]

There are many ways to read church history and the Reformation, but as we look to the future we are going to need some extra help, which might require learning to see ourselves from a different angle. Since each division of the church could be seen as a divorce, it's appropriate we learn from the growing field of marriage therapy for insights into our collective healing. To be blunt, the field of marriage therapy and family systems can help us pray the prayer of John 17, that we would be one as Jesus and the Father are one. If we are to be the family of

God, maybe family systems theory could help us. Specifically, the growing research and wisdom on differentiation could prove useful as we seek to connect with other Christians in our everyday life.

In *The Passionate Marriage*, marriage therapist David Schnarch begins with a head-turning premise about what marriage is for or what the goal of marriage is. Many people would say it's companionship, falling in love, nurturing that love, creating the capacity for a family, and all the stuff in the movies. While every romantic movie includes the happy ceremony of vows, that blissful feeling of being lost in each other's gaze and floating just above the surface of the ground, Schnarch says this has nothing to do with being married. Schnarch calls marriage "a people growing machine."[3] In other words, marriage is not meant to be an arrival but a process of confronting reality and growing up as a people, which happens best in a committed relationship.

It's a very similar dynamic for a local church. Whether we realize it or not, being married is a promise we make to grow up. At the heart of this endeavor to grow up is the never-ending journey of differentiation. Essentially, this is "the ability to hold onto yourself while maintaining relationships with others."[4] Just as this is the case in a marriage, this is how Jesus-following groups, teams, and even congregations should think and act at the local level. The questions for our culture-creating teams are: Who are we? What are we about? And how do we stay connected with teams different from us?

Church splits could be transformed when, just like marriage, we see the church as a people-growing machine, not an institution to make us happy. The goal is maturity, wholeness, and shalom, not self-actualization. By shifting the narrative of the purpose of the church, we might already be on our way. I know this might seem too simple for such a complex problem, but when an individual church or an entire denomination changes, it changes the collective relationship. A line is either explicitly or implicitly drawn in the sand, and a reaction is prompted. Either both parties learn how to be in the relationship in a new way and grow, or they do not and separate. At least three things are needed for both parties to transform:

- ✦ They cannot be led by the old narrative that the church exists for ourselves.
- ✦ Both parties need to further clarify who they are.
- ✦ Both parties need to learn how to embrace and connect through their particularity, not in spite of it.

What would happen if we collectively decided that this will be our new stance? What if instead of dividing, we used our differences to further clarify who we are and how we can uniquely contribute to God's hope for the place we share? We cannot do this without limitations. But if we receive the gift of our geographic limitation, we can begin to work toward our identity as particular teams that stay connected in a growing web of belonging and relationship. If we don't embrace our unique calling in our unique contexts, I fear we will simply mirror our increasingly polarized culture rather than learning how to trust God that another way is possible.

Tribal Mob Versus Same Team

There are legitimate reasons to fear that Western society increasingly resembles a mob. Our entrenched ideology is fueled by a social media landscape that rewards fighting harder and louder. With more fights and more attention, the ratings go up and the ad revenue grows. This is the perfect business model to enhance the seductive tribal story.

But the feeling of belonging experienced by vilifying the other side will not sustain us. We might feel close because of our shared hatred for some other category: the immigrants, the Muslims, the evangelicals, the Republicans, the greedy capitalists, or the needy socialists. Whatever label we produce for the others, it is not a fruit of the Spirit. Brené Brown explains that shame cannot be used as a tool of liberation. The moment that we categorize people as "other," we are playing into the hands of the enemy. The tribe feels intimate, it feels like a movement, but it cannot last. The grand challenge of our day, which is part of God's call, is to learn how to function as a team even though we have astounding differences and in spite of all the profound forces pulling us apart.

If we dare think of ourselves as on the same team, then we need to change the rules of the game a little bit. The game is to join in what God is doing in our parish; therefore we can all get after it. As long as we are competing with one another for the attention and tithing dollars of the faithful, we will sacrifice the long game. Don't get me wrong: tragedies like the sexual abuse scandals or the continual power-hungry egos we see in so many religious circles are horrific and should be faced, mourned, and transformed. But it's also damaging to our witness when we believe and act as though we are on dramatically different teams. Officially, we might treat one another with respect, as competitive companies do, but at our worst we treat one another with contempt.

The church needs to recover what it means to be on the same team, to recover our vocation to be the body of Christ. But for that to be possible, we need to come together in the same place. If we dare to imagine that we could be one body, including our limits and responsibilities—one dream of God—we need one place to practice in. Our culture is screaming for this kind of movement. It's hard to read the newspaper and not see our broader culture begging for a team of people to become the bridge builders, the peacemakers, the defenders of the *imago Dei* present in every single person.

Change the Game, Don't Let the Game Change You

The old game of church competition won't allow for the kind of collaboration we need. When the church itself is the main thing, it usually means that every theological and cultural difference becomes a threat. "If they are right, we must be wrong." We need to find a relationally driven grassroots approach to the clear command of Jesus in John 17. I'm not trying to downplay the serious and legitimate differences that are splitting the church into ever-increasing factions. These differences are real, they matter, and they have a real impact. To pretend like we are all the same or that we should just do our best to get along will not lead to the transformation we need. It will not work to ignore the differences. But when we can see how our differences play out in real time with our actual neighbors, we are on much better footing to address the reality of differences. At the neighborhood level, where the primary task is to discern God's dreams, these deeply help theological and cultural differences can be worked out on the ground, where we can feel the effects of our actions.

Unity Versus Uniformity

My friend and colleague Jonathan Brooks often speaks about the drastic difference between unity and uniformity.[5] Unity is achieved when we see the *imago Dei* in one another, when we refuse to live by the cultural script that some lives have more value than others. Unity thus honors diversity. Unity requires vigilant curiosity, a common story, and the kind of humility that most of us (myself included) do not value. When we show our neighborhood that we are united in spite of our differences, then we can embody the grand reuniting that Christ makes possible. Jesus clearly says that this will be how other people see and experience the love of God. This unity is not the equivalent of divine instruction to eat our vegetables; there is nothing peripheral about this urgent command. It's about a lot more than our reputation as a Christian community; it's our lives showcasing what we believe to be true of God.

We also shouldn't try to cheapen it with *uniformity* (i.e., all need to be the same if we are going to get along). The call for uniformity is a classic strategy of the majority with deep roots in the logic of colonization. It's a dangerous substitute to the unity we are commanded to work toward. We cannot legislate from the top down the type of reconnection we hope will transpire. Our question is this: Is there a way forward that models unity without uniformity?

The only way we can begin to model unity, not uniformity, is at the local level in our everyday lives. When we have the courage to say that we are on the same team and that the game is not getting people to come to our services but to listen for what God is doing and figure it out together, we will have changed the game. The old game is pretty simple. Argue abstract theological and political philosophies. If we are honest, this is where the splits begin. But just like in divorce court, the real battle lies with money, property, legacy, and power politics. We simply cannot afford to keep playing by these rules. Insanity is sometimes described as doing the same thing over and over again and hoping for a different result. I'm pretty convinced that our primary strategies for church unity are insane.

We can, of course, keep doing what we are presently doing. We can fight on Twitter, ignore each other, and give up. Resignation just might be the Achilles' heel of this generation moving into leadership. In the face of all these ridiculous challenges, when everything is melting down, when our politics, economics, and primary cultural narratives are essentially up for grabs, we will be tempted to shrug, refresh Instagram, and toss in the towel.

God is calling us to change this game. Assuming we can discover the church right where we are, we can show others that another way is possible. When we learn to see the church in our everyday life, it won't provide easy answers, but we cannot unsee it either. It's one thing to say that it's impossible and cannot be attempted. It's entirely different to say we will need to absolutely depend on God to have a chance of seeing this happen. To say unity is impossible is effectively to say the gospel is not true. Powerful forces want us to give up. The powers that be do not want to see a movement of hopeful resistance. They do not want us to change the story. They do not want curiosity and courage to lead the way. They want us to shut up, get in line, and buy more stuff. This story of resignation cannot win.

What would happen if over the next few decades we collectively decided to pursue a new vision of becoming unified? I'm not talking about getting an impressive delegation to go to Rome, though that would be interesting. What if, over the next few decades, we made a turn toward curiosity, shared purpose, and shared potential based on God's work in our actual common ground? The bridge between real differences would be the commitment to loving God and our neighbors. This would transform us in a way that we might not be able to fathom.

We can't be on the same team the way we are playing the game right now. In fact, if we keep playing by these rules, the number of denominations will only increase over the next few decades. If we can figure out how to be on the same team at the neighborhood level, grow trust, and begin to tell a new story, we can be a signpost of the reconciliation we are meant to embody. As it happens in one neighborhood, it will spread to others. While there is no finish line to this endeavor, there will be profound breakthroughs to celebrate. There will be moments to mark when we feel like we are doing this well, but the very next day it might feel like it's going to fall apart. The key will be to keep the long game in mind and trust God with what is possible.

Walking Together

In many of Seattle's neighborhoods, gentrification and displacement of longtime residents is a major concern. Within the changing context of the Hillman City neighborhood, two churches that care passionately about the neighborhood are rooting themselves there and doing what they can to collaborate. One is a United Methodist church, which is more progressive, and the other is a Free Methodist church, which means it broke off from the UMC ages ago. They are good examples of starting down the path of being on the same team even though their history, their systems, and their doctrinal statements differ. According to the old game, these two congregations should not be on speaking terms. But because they are both deeply committed to the shalom of God in the neighborhood, they realize they need to figure out what it means for them to be on the same team. I don't want to over-romanticize this. Though it's hard, it is possible because of their shared desire and shared context.

David Leong is an elder at Rainer Avenue Church, which is the Free Methodist church, and John Helmiere is the founding pastor of Valley and Mountain United Methodist Church. Through mutual appreciation, curiosity, and a shared geographic context, they have learned to collaborate beautifully. Their relationship is slowly knitting these congregations together without making either of them capitulate to the other. In his work as a professor of missiology at Seattle Pacific University, David repeatedly takes students to learn from what is happening with Valley and Mountain. John has also learned quite a bit from David's critical work on race, place, and missiology. There isn't the need to do everything together, but these are two of the most visible churches in the neighborhood, and if they didn't talk to each other or, worse, if they only talked trash about each other, then that would profoundly tarnish the witness of God's work in the neighborhood. Over time, more trust is being built, and a new story is beginning to emerge.

Dwight Friesen often says that it's impossible for institutions to collaborate. This might sound like a linguistic trick, but organizations cannot collaborate—only the people within them do. This is a journey we can embrace whether or not we hold a leadership position at our faith community. We need to begin where there is a desire to see this possibility of unity grow.

In figure 6.1, the first circle represents the core team that is telling a new story and committing to a way of life together. The second circle is meant to show how the invisible church in the neighborhood can become more visible and journey together.

Figure 6.1. Journeying together

The journey I'm proposing would grow from a small team of commitment to a larger team of relationships. We move from a culture-making core to a growing neighborhood movement, but that movement is based on a common place rather than a common service. The word *congregation* is most appropriate for this first team, which is synonymous with an expression of the local church. The dream is that the entire church, all the followers of Christ in a given place, would over time find unique ways to join together in God's dreams for that place. While the idea of a congregation, at least how we think of one, would have been present in the letters to the early Christians of the New Testament era, the *ecclesia* or the gathered ones in that place would have been seen as the church of Colossae, Corinth, Galatia, and so forth. What held these churches together was their confession that Jesus is Lord, their trust that the Spirit was at work among them, and their life together within a geographical area. What could happen if this was our goal as well?

If the mission of God is reconciliation, but the church is not reconciled at the local level, then prioritizing unity is not an add-on but the very core of the mission of God. Essentially, our culture has been calling our bluff for good reason. The biblical message is reconciliation between God, creation, and ourselves, but because we can't stay in the same room together, perhaps we shouldn't be believed. Since the underlying issues tearing us apart are isolation, polarization, and fragmentation, we need to cultivate practices that subvert them, even from within the Christian community. This is a pathway we should at least explore. To get there, the following are three practices for the core team to experiment with as they seek to knit the local church together in their parish.

From isolation to awareness. If our primary posture is defensive, do something to learn a bit more about one another. How about a meal or a cup of coffee? Ask new questions of one another and practice the art of appreciative inquiry. There are so many ways that we can lead with and receive hospitality. I'm not proposing that we need to get coffee with every single Christian we meet, but it sure would be good to get to know as many followers of Christ as possible.

From polarization to curiosity. Every time we lean in with curiosity, we are growing our chances to showcase the love of God to our neighbors. Tragically, the reverse is true too. Each cold shoulder, each disparaging remark, each side-glance of contempt for their backward theological position does lasting damage. I'm guilty of this. You might be too. The task is not to do this perfectly in one triumphant gathering but to knit together social capital among the Christians in the neighborhood so we join in God's transformation together. This is why it's so critical to have a small team that builds the culture. As we keep connecting at the speed of trust, I think we will be astounded by the stories we get to see transpire.

✦ Who is there?

✦ What are they up to?

✦ How are they sensing God at work in the neighborhood?

✦ What is their tradition?

✦ What is it like for them to follow Jesus in this place?

From fragmentation to integration. The journey together will most likely take a while. It has taken centuries for our churches to quit trusting one another. Even worse, we have built entire systems to keep us apart. With this in mind, we shouldn't expect to see massive change quickly. We would be wiser to become far more aware, become much more curious, and then take small, achievable steps together and build from there. It might be helpful to note that different kinds of relationships have different levels of intimacy. The goal is to begin to move from being strangers to becoming acquaintances and then friends that share a common story in our shared Christian faith. So, begin to ask, What could we do together? Think small, then think smaller. What might be possible if we try something together? Are there challenges or opportunities that none of us could do on our own but we could with a much larger team? What experiments would both delight God and one another? What are the ways we could avoid duplication? How can we pray for one another? What can we do to eat together more often? How do we learn to celebrate one another?

These are not complicated ideas, but if this became a way of life for us, we would see a new movement in our day.

CHAPTER SEVEN

LEARNING FROM LOCAL HEROES

We become what we behold.

WILLIAM BLAKE

B elieve it or not, when we are strolling through a forest, we are surrounded by a conversation between the trees. It's true. Just because we experience silence in the forest doesn't mean there's not a conversation taking place all around us.

Seriously! When we walk in the woods we might be amid a lively conversation. Emerging scientific studies suggest this to be true, but we can't listen closely enough to hear it. The conversation is largely happening through scent in the air and beneath our feet. While trees don't communicate quickly, they do release "scent compounds that are specifically formulated for the task at hand."[1] Especially if there is danger, trees inform one another through scents carried along by the breeze signaling a common threat. Another way they can communicate is through "chemical signals sent through fungal networks around their root tips." Quite literally, the roots can talk to one another through the vast network of interconnections, which author Peter Wohlleben cheekily calls the "wood-wide web."[2]

There is almost always more going on than meets the eye. It turns out trees are far more social than most of us were taught. Just because we can't see (or hear or smell) something doesn't mean there isn't something profound happening. The key is to learn how to see in new ways. It's difficult to see something if we aren't looking for it. It shouldn't surprise us that when we learn to ask new questions and explore in new ways, we'll be delightfully shocked at what we discover.

What We Behold We Become

James and Deborah Fallows felt like they needed to learn how to see in a new way. Both were accomplished writers who felt they needed to pursue different kinds of stories. They were used to reading and even writing from the frenzy of Washington, DC. So they set out on a multiyear tour across dozens of smaller cities to take a "fresh look at the country, its disappointments and opportunities."[3] They seemed to be asking, Are there places where people are learning how to talk to one another, to come together around shared values in the public arena? Is it really as bad as the headlines keep telling us?

Their extended journey through the United States led to an important book called *Our Town*, which became a travelogue manifesto of hundreds of stories worth celebrating. With James as the pilot in their small Cessna, over several years they embarked on dozens of trips to small towns to try to discern what was really happening on the ground. Time and again they discovered stories that contradicted the fearful narratives they had heard. From Holland, Michigan, to Fresno, California, local heroes were devoting their lives to their communities. They were overwhelmed by the quantity and the quality of these citizens everywhere they went.

They found that despite what we all keep reading about on Facebook and in the news, resilient, innovative people were doing all sorts of beautiful things. The first major shift in their thinking arose from how they viewed the world; they were on a quest for hope, not for headlines. Their second insight was that the closer they got to the ground, the easier it was to identify the people working hard to contribute to the common good of their shared context.

We can have the same experience. If the headlines have us convinced that everything is falling apart and getting a whole lot worse with every passing week, we might be surprised when we listen for hopeful stories in ordinary places. We should not be swept away by the noise that's blaring at us from the top down. We all know the political playbook of stoking fears and putting the spotlight on polarizing problems to rally the base. That is the easy path of clichéd sound bites. Tragically, it's possible our faith communities have slipped into using the same strategies. If we want to get national attention, this might be a fabulous playbook. But to cultivate and grow a movement, we need to get as close to the ground as we can and pay close attention. We need to be on the hunt not for "what's wrong, but what is strong" in our neighborhoods.[4] Hope is rising from neighborhoods throughout the world, if only we have the eyes to see it.

By simply walking around our neighborhoods and being on the lookout for the gifts and skills and hopes of others, we will be shocked at the abundance of ordinary heroes at the grassroots level. There is a direct relationship between how close to the ground we are getting and our reasons for hope.

If we are looking for signs of hope, not only do we need to get a lot more local, we obviously need to look at all of our neighbors. Some will read this as patently obvious, and I imagine others have sincere questions about it. Stay with me for a bit because there is too much at stake in discerning where we look for hope. We cannot afford to allow fear to win the day. When our primary posture to others, to our very own neighbors, is fear or indifference, it's almost always a clue that we are not orienting our lives to the gospel of Jesus, which changes everything. In times of massive change and fragmentation, it's easy to let fear win the day. There are sobering challenges ahead, but we can't lead with fear.

The Benedict Option and Karl Marx

The Benedict Option received more press than just about any book on the church in the past few decades. A more public conversation about the church just doesn't happen very often. This book struck a cultural nerve. Part of the reason it made such an impact stems from an unlikely comparison. While author Rod Dreher is a self-described conservative, as I read his book I kept thinking about a common remark I often heard in regard to Karl Marx's famous book The Communist Manifesto. Both are extremely insightful and even prophetic in their analysis, but they suffer in their prescription for the future.

Dreher does a brilliant job of walking us through the story of how things got to this cultural moment in which secularism and individualism seem to reign supreme. Marx, of course, emerged as an influential critic of capitalism run amok. Both pinpoint the fact that something is very wrong here. There are good reasons to be afraid: that is not in dispute. However, I contend that by reacting in fear we can't build a new strategy without compounding fear. In the case of *The Benedict Option*, the call is for a strategic retreat of Christians from the distorting effects of individualism and secularism.

The issue, however, is not about retreating versus advancing; it's not about our techniques for change but trusting God no matter where we are. The question is not whether we should be more conservative or progressive, but where we are placing our hope and trust. Do we trust God or ourselves? This is the moment-by-moment question we struggle with. It's not solely an intellectual decision we make about who God is and what God has done. It's a living, breathing, always-before-us question.

The "Benedict option" of hunkering down seems to point to hope, but because it's rooted in our reaction rather than God's activity, I'm afraid it will take us off course. As I read *The Benedict Option*, I was struck by how much human agency was involved rather than God's activity. At the extreme end, it could almost be interpreted that God isn't active in the lives of our neighbors.

We don't need to be afraid of our neighbors; we need to learn from them. Christians do not have the market cornered on being kind, generous, or loving. The fruits of the Spirit are on display in all sorts of people. The decision to retreat in order to escape the unjust and increasingly post-Christian climate misses an extremely important reality. When we have the eyes to see, many of our neighbors will teach us how to follow Jesus by their own examples. Pastor Tim Keller speaks of this as "common grace," the fact that "God gives out gifts of wisdom, talent, beauty, and skill according to his grace—that is, in a completely unmerited way. He casts them across the human race like seed, in order to enrich, brighten, and preserve the world." He also notes that if we forget this reality, then "Christians can believe they can live self-sufficiently within their own cultural enclave."[5]

We don't need to retreat from the "godless" culture, we need to be present alongside our neighbors who are already loving and serving the neighborhood. The different trajectories of these small decisions have the potential to shape the church in dramatic ways. How we see our neighbors will profoundly affect the future of the church. If we are essentially fearful of the other, then that is what we are likely to become. While strategic retreat has historic precedent within various monastic orders, I believe that it misses the truth that we actually need our neighbors in order to discern how we are to follow Jesus. It also violates an ecological principle of diversity we see in God's good creation.

Monoculture Leads to Death

Within each of our places we are called to be faithfully present to the diversity of thought, experience, and wisdom. This is a gift to be received rather than a threat. The tendency to retreat into a holy huddle will get us in trouble.

For many years, while facilitating learning communities for the Parish Collective, I've brought parish leaders to visit hundreds of neighborhoods. One of the most interesting fieldtrips we take is in rural Newberg, Oregon, at Eloheh Farms, the home of Randy and Edith Woodley. Randy, a respected missiologist, and Edith have welcomed hundreds of people to their farm, not just for rich conversation but also for an embodied experience of how theology connects with Native American traditions, biomimicry (how we learn from what God has made), and permaculture (designing plants and space to grow well together and replenish the soil). These ancient practices have profound relevance for us today. As you might imagine, their farm is bursting with life. All sorts of plants are growing together in a designed cacophony of abundance. It brings joy to be there and witness what's possible when we look for the interdependence inherent in nature.

It's also just as shocking to see what surrounds their farm. Just beyond their front porch and wrapping around much of their property is a walnut farm: row after row of walnut trees with nothing growing underneath them. These trees are heavily reinforced with chemical pesticides that make the Woodleys sick when the trees are sprayed. The monoculture we see of big agriculture with gallons of pesticides might be more manageable and even yield more filbert nuts, but it's not nearly as resilient and will eventually deplete the soil.

I hope you see my point. We are called to be light, to be yeast, to be fit together with our neighbors, not to shield ourselves from them. The truth is that we likely have more to learn from them than we have to teach.

We can see from a more ecological perspective that we can do more together in relationships than we can apart. Moreover, we learn how to piece this together by looking at the strengths each plant brings to the whole rather than to its deficits. We can do the same in most other areas.

From What's Wrong to What's Strong

Somehow I have mistakenly been formed to see most people through the eyes of Genesis 3 rather than Genesis 1. I think this happened through osmosis—the slow, cumulative effect of growing up in an evangelical culture. Here's what I mean. In the beginning God created *everything*—and it was good. By the time the creation story comes to human beings, the text says that we were not merely "good" but "very good." We need to begin here with every human being. It's hard work, but if we can't see the image of God in each neighbor, each friend, each politician, each person, then we don't have good news to offer. Yes, we are all marred by sin. Yes, it's difficult to be human. But we need to lean in to the idea that "the shadow proves the sunshine" rather than the other way around.[6]

Making sure we start at the beginning of the story has enormous implications, but the reverse is not just some fringe idea that has settled into Christian culture. It's far more pervasive in pretty much all of the helping industries. Isn't it true that nearly all social services and nonprofits start by identifying and seeking to address deficiencies and needs? These industries stem from the good desire to help, but this doesn't mean it's the framework we should use to connect with our neighbors.

Usually, in our good desire to help, we begin with a fatal flaw. When we label and define people by what they lack or need instead of by the gifts and skills they possess, we subtly read their lives from the vantage point of Genesis 3. We inadvertently label people fundamentally as rebellious sinners worthy of judgment *before we see them as the good creation of God.* This isn't done with malicious intent, but without meaning to we can easily hurt people in our attempt to help.

While there is no fail-safe way to engage in a relationship without the risk of pain and harm, we can choose to view our neighbors either through the lens of abundance or scarcity. But can we embody good news as a team when we are focused on what's wrong with our neighbors? When we decide to look for assets rather than needs, the implications are illuminating. Rather than looking at a neighborhood's needs and problems, what if we instead look for the gifts and strengths of people and the places where they reside?

Focusing on what's strong instead of what's wrong has dramatic implications. Table 7.1, often used when highlighting "asset-based community development," shows divergent trajectories.

Table 7.1. Needs-based versus gifts-based approaches

NEEDS	GIFTS
Problem to solve	People
Program to create	Relationship to grow
Professional to manage	Communities to encourage
Consumers of help	Citizens of promise

Within the larger complex of people and organizations who are hoping to be helpful, it's unfortunately true that just because we want to be helpful doesn't mean we actually are. Intention does not always result in the impact we'd like to have—it's just not that easy.

As we seek to be a team that is coming together to discern God's dreams for our neighborhood, we can still cause damage to our neighbors, which is even more likely when we are approaching them with a needs-based or deficit-based approach.

We must not see our neighbors as either people to be feared or a project to be managed by professionals. What if our growing team, the people who are becoming the church in the neighborhood, decided that their primary approach to their neighbors was to listen for the gifts and skills and strengths of each person? We would not only have the opportunity to champion and celebrate them, but we could be the connective tissue between these ordinary heroes.

Just like Jesus says, "those who want to save their life will lose it, but those who lose their life for my sake will find it" (Matthew 16:25). This ancient wisdom is available to us today in our frenetic, marketed, image-driven culture. Let's learn how to collectively give ourselves away to Jesus and his mission and see our gifted and skilled neighbors as participants in this mission. We just might discover who we were meant to be by weaving a fabric of care and trust between all the amazing people in the neighborhood who are not yet connected, supported, and championed.

De'Amon Harges and Mike Mather beautifully embody how powerful learning from our neighbors can be for an entire congregation. Mike is the senior pastor of Broadway United Methodist Church in Indianapolis. Years ago, he invited De'Amon to reframe the church's entire outreach approach by "focusing our efforts on what is present rather than what is not." Over time, something profound shifted. In his excellent book *Having Nothing, Possessing Everything*, Mike writes, "More than developing great church programming, we were developing new patterns of church, new ways of being neighbors.

We were trying to see what was right in front of us, hidden in plain sight."[7] This invitation is open to all of us.

Up to this point we have examined how we can connect with, learn from, and build trust with our courageous Christian neighbors. Now we need to expand our horizon to the third circle (see fig. 7.1). While dozens may commit to being on a culture-shaping team, and hundreds of Christians share the same story, there are likely thousands of citizens around us with tremendous gifts, skills, and hopes that can be connected to God's dream in the neighborhood. They might not be motivated by God's dream in Scripture for all things to be reconciled, but that doesn't mean they can't be characters of this story. When we see the fruit of the Spirit (Galatians 5:22-23) within our neighbors, when we see their passion for justice, when we see them creating beauty and hospitality, we should be the first to celebrate it. The following are some practical ways we can begin.

Map assets. While we are connecting with the core team and also with the growing roster of Christians in the neighborhood, we need to map the assets. I think everyone will be astonished by the quantity and quality of people, associations, businesses, nonprofits, and even government agencies that are contributing to the flourishing of life in their neighborhood. Get a huge map and place pins on it to chronicle the many people and organizations the team can learn from and perhaps join. Get creative

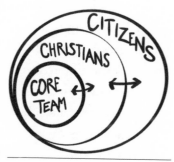

Figure 7.1. Unconnected citizens

with it. Compile photos and images of the neighbors, buildings, and logos of organizations as a huge collage. Also make a spreadsheet of all the incredible people and organizations in the neighborhood. This joyful work won't ever stop, but it does lead beautifully to the second practice.

Champion heroes. It feels amazing when someone sees something in you that you also love about yourself. When we care about something and are committed to it, we aren't doing it for praise or attention. But sometimes, if we're honest, we wonder if anyone is noticing, if any of it really matters. This is a pretty normal human predicament. What if the Christians in the neighborhood became known for naming the gifts, strengths, and hopes of others? What if we got creative with how we champion and celebrate others? We could create neighborhood awards and be extravagant with our praise of others. What if we became advocates for one another and brag about each other in the local press? Let's buy our neighbors coffee and tell them why they matter so much to us and what we are learning from them.

Ask more questions. If the Christians in the neighborhood became known more for the quality of our questions rather than our answers, we would see a dramatic shift in how people engage the Christian faith. And, naturally, we will want to learn more from them. What if we ask them not just about their expertise but also their motivations? Open-ended questions will help us understand where they are coming from. We could start local podcasts and listening sessions, and from what we learn, perhaps our neighbors will help us to better follow Jesus. Just imagine how the tide could turn if we were known for our gratitude and curiosity instead of judgment and certainty.

Bono, the lead singer of the band U2, once confessed he spent a lot of his time asking God to bless what he was doing. Then he realized the order was wrong. A pastor friend told him, "Stop asking God to bless what you're doing. Find out what God's doing. It's already blessed."[8]

Pretty good advice, huh? Perhaps the church could learn from this. Rather than starting everything ourselves so we can own it, what if we were the team of people who were encouraging, supporting, and championing every single beautiful thing in the neighborhood?

I hope you can feel that by seeing our neighbors through the lens of abundance, an entirely new journey unfolds. It's a journey God is calling us to today.

CHAPTER EIGHT

ALREADY HERE

The future is already here,
it's just not well distributed.

WILLIAM GIBSON

E very kid wants their parents to be proud of them. It's also true that every parent wants to pass wisdom on to their children. There are all sorts of ways this can happen. Most parents have probably experienced how this happens most profoundly as their kids watch their actual lives. As Albert Schweitzer said, "Example is not the main thing in influencing others, it's the only thing."[1] More than what we teach, how we navigate our adversities and joys ends up being the primary classroom for our kids. This is true of a remarkable professor most people have never heard of, and his simple graph that has changed the world.

Everett Rogers was born in rural Iowa in 1931, during the Great Depression. Each year, Everett's father had to decide which variety of corn to plant. While he was interested in the advances in electricity and new farming equipment, he was far more resistant to adopting the latest corn-seed hybrid innovation. He was afraid these new seeds wouldn't yield as much corn as tried-and-true varieties had in years past, so he stayed the course and used the seeds he had used the previous year. Unfortunately for the Rogers family, this decision would have serious implications.

As a five-year-old in 1936, sweet little Everett would have been old enough to help with small tasks on the farm. He certainly would have witnessed the major drought of that summer. Many years later, his father's resistance to risk and change would be the catalyst of a simple bell curve that has influenced thousands of leaders in nearly every sector of society.

Because of the decision not to plant the new seeds, a slow and catastrophic picture began to unfold during the great drought of 1936. Day by day the Rogers family watched their precious corn wilt and die. Making matters worse, they were surrounded by neighboring farms whose corn stood tall and strong because they bought into the newer, more resilient seed varietal. Everett's dad paid an extremely high price for his choice not to use the new seed. Everett Rogers grew up with the painful reminder that how quickly a new idea is adopted can have real consequences. Eventually, this thought transformed how thousands of leaders think about change and how it can be led.

You've probably heard of the "innovation curve." It's a simple bell shape that's been used in nearly every sector of our society to better understand how new ideas and projects tend to either grow and become the norm or never make an impact.

Through the innovation curve, Rogers showed how ideas, products, and even movements generally progress from the earliest stage to building up steam and becoming the new norm. He coined the term *early adopter*, which designates the 13.5 percent of people who are the first wave to buy into a new idea or product. For example, those who are early adopters of technology might have purchased an iPhone within the first few months it came out in 2007.

If an idea or product builds up steam, we move from the early adopters to the early majority, then on to the late majority, and finally to the laggards. The laggards, for example, are the people who, perhaps wisely, resist getting a smartphone even though most others have.

This is a crucial framework for us to use because it helps map where we might be and how we might be able to move forward. Perhaps the first place to start is to remind ourselves that the practical imagination of the church is essentially up for grabs. The ideas that now seem so far out there and perhaps impossible might be patently obvious in just a few decades.

Seth Godin notes, "Things that are accepted now, things that virtually everyone believes in as universal, timeless truths, were fringe practices a century or less ago."[2] The innovation curve profoundly affects how Seth thinks, writes, and creates. In nearly all innovation and entrepreneurial sectors, the majority of leaders have been profoundly influenced by Everett Rogers's work even if they don't know his name. Discerning where we might be on the innovation curve helps us listen with far better acuity to the desires and fears of those who have yet to be convinced. It also helps us understand how we can create experiences and environments that build momentum. We gain this type of traction by knowing what kinds of hopes and questions people might be asking, based on where they are located on the curve.

A key place to begin is to discern who the roughly 15 percent are that are eager to take a risk. Then the roughly 70 percent waiting to see if it works, and finally who are the 15 percent who will be resistant to any change. People will be at different points of this curve for all sorts of reasons. The defining piece of wisdom is to discern where they are on the curve and who they are listening to. The story of Everett Rogers's father reveals both the complexity and impact of our posture toward change. He wasn't against all technology, but he resisted the new seed varieties until it was too late. He may have paid a price for being late to the game, but that doesn't mean he didn't have good reasons for resisting. This frame of reference helps us map the relationship that people have to any given change. And if we want to help lead change, we need to have a sense of where we are at in the overall picture.

The movement of new ideas along is complex, but it typically has three common elements:

1. The idea takes time to mature and adapt.

2. The idea travels by word of mouth; it's a grassroots movement of peers.

3. New people don't just hear about it, they get to experience it.

A remarkable opportunity is set before us over the next few decades. While there will be no silver bullet for the church, if we learn how to connect across our neighborhoods and learn from one another, we'll discover that in weaving our stories and experiences together, we have everything we need.

This connecting, which is already underway, will strengthen the movement that is building steam right at this very moment.

It won't grow through a slick advertising campaign but from everyday people experimenting and sharing their stories. The way to move across this innovation curve is through connecting. We begin connecting with early adopters, then the early majority, and so on. But as Geoffrey A. Moore has pointed out in *Crossing the Chasm*, at each stage of the innovation curve there is an invisible chasm, a new space that must be crossed.[3] If we want to grow a movement, we need to realize that each section is asking fundamentally different questions based on where they are located.

The Compound Interest of Presence

In his stunning book *The Patient Ferment of the Early Church*, Mennonite scholar Alan Kreider has a surprising thesis about why the early church grew so quickly.[4] The title of the book hints at the main idea, but it doesn't tell us why the early church was so profoundly patient. After all, how can people make patience their highest priority when they literally might lose their lives for their beliefs? Kreider claims the early church grew so rapidly and affected nearly every aspect of society because they lived by an alternative story in the public square. They placed their hope in the firm belief that God was at work and would bring about the future. When we put these two realities together over a few centuries and add the crucial ingredient of sharing wisdom and stories of faith across places, we begin to see how the early church began to experience the compound interest of faithful presence. Essentially, their witness moved others along the innovation curve.

Playing the Long Game

One of my favorite parts of Parish Collective gatherings is hearing the courageous neighborhood stories of friends from all around the world. At the beginning of our first Cultivate Gathering in February 2019, I heard the story of Kindra Green Carson of the City Heights neighborhood of San Diego. She struggled to come to grips with the injustice of a massage parlor that was obviously trafficking women in her neighborhood. Thankfully, her prayerful persistence and presence eventually resulted in justice, but it was her time horizon that so affected me. It took a ten-year commitment, not just a few, for Kindra to witness God's victory in this situation. When we think in terms of decades rather than years, it changes our posture of what can happen. It helps to settle us into the patient work of God and opens us to see how much change is possible. When we think about months or a few years, our imaginations are stunted.

If the game is joining God in the holistic restoration and renewal of a place, we shouldn't get our hearts set on this happening in a few years. It's going to take a while. It's also going to be difficult, which probably doesn't come as a surprise. If we don't have other communities of practice that can celebrate what is happening, if we don't receive the wisdom of others, and if we don't grow from the experience of communities that have been at this for far longer than we have, we are going to struggle to stay present and active over the long haul. There is no short game in seeking to be the church in our everyday lives; it's all a long game, which means we need one another more than ever.

If I were to offer you a million dollars today or a penny which doubles each day for a month, which would you choose? While it would be awfully difficult to pass up a million dollars, it would be the wrong choice. If you chose the penny, after two weeks you'd still only have $81.92 and feel like you made a horrible mistake. But if you waited to the end of the month you would have $5,357,709.[5] That is the magic of compound interest. I believe a similar dynamic is true for our presence in neighborhoods. The potential is enormous, but earlier on it's vulnerable and might not look successful.

In Seattle there are forty neighborhoods (though boundaries and names are always fluctuating). If a team of ten people joined God's work in each neighborhood and had the capacity to connect these neighborhoods, making them far more resilient and innovative, God would produce forty different church expressions totaling four hundred people. Contrast this with a regional church of four thousand attendees drawing from all forty of these neighborhoods but with no focused presence in those neighborhoods. If we compared these two over ten years, which would have a more profound effect? I'd put all my chips on the forty smaller expressions. This has nothing to do with them being small but with their desire and capacity to learn from one another. If we could match this ten-year period with the innovation that comes from peer learning, the fermentation of a movement would bubble up. The question then becomes, How do we help accelerate change by making connections both within and across our neighborhoods?

The quality of change we are seeking will likely be slow —until it hits a tipping point. The visual language of fermentation is helpful because of how it progresses. There is a slow build; transformation is underway but happening just out of sight. The status quo appears to be winning the day, but something else is bubbling up to the surface. There is no obvious clue that massive transformation is just underneath the surface, but that doesn't mean it's not there. A reformation might be brewing right beneath the surface.

New Ideas from New Places

By connecting across neighborhoods and celebrating the stories of what's possible, we are putting ourselves in an excellent position to experience innovation. How good ideas grow is of special interest to writer Steven Johnson. Specifically, he has been on a quest to discern what environments best produce good ideas. In seeking answers to this excellent question, he downplays the notion that ideas spring out of nowhere. Brilliant ideas look more like a network. In fact, that's much closer to what is happening inside our brain. An idea is not a brand new thing that comes from nowhere but rather the result of what happens when multiple thoughts converge. "A new idea is produced by a new network of neurons firing in sync with each other. It's a new configuration that's never been formed before."[6] When we connect with another community that's committed to their parish, we are creating an environment for innovation. By connecting our common practices within contrasting contexts, we are setting the stage for an unlimited number of new ideas.

I've never loved the phrase "outside the box," as though new thoughts, images, or products magically appear apart from any context, system, or structure. A far better way for us to think about innovation is to look at what is possible on the "edge of the box." We are still connected to our real lives and the present systems and structures. But we are leaning off the edge toward what is possible. When two faith communities haven't left their boxes but each is on the edge of its box in order to connect to the other, new insights, ideas, and encouragement will be produced.

If we can get a few friends who are committed to joining God in their parish to meet up with another small team in a different neighborhood and they walk around their neighborhoods and share stories, we will sow the seeds of revolution. Reading about other communities, watching videos, and checking websites can be helpful, but nothing comes close to learning from others in their own context. As philosopher Michael Polanyi famously said, "We can know more than we can tell."[7] By putting our bodies in new contexts we learn and grow in ways we can't quite put into words.

As we take in the sights, smells, and feelings of being in a new place, we'll also reflect on the differences from our own place. Even better, if this is a shared experience with people on our team, then we'll get multiple observations and perspectives. All these intersections heighten the opportunity for the innovation that is needed right now. The observations of new places also give us another precious gift: a chance to glimpse some of our own blind spots.

Helping to Name Our Blind Spots

If you didn't see my headshot on the back cover of this book, you might not know that I am a white man. But you can't see just how white I am. I love the Chicago Cubs. My favorite outside activities are surfing, sailing, and hiking. My all-time favorite band is U2. My go-to beer is a strong IPA. I think you get the gist.[8]

Is there anything wrong with any of these things? No, of course not. But there is something wrong with thinking that what I like and what makes me comfortable should be the standard for everyone else. While it's true that my beloved wife has helped me to see how white I am, I've learned even more by being in different neighborhoods and receiving the hospitality of people who are different from me. This can be true for our communities as well. Yes, we all inhabit a particular culture. But our blind spots, which can do real harm to others, will remain that way until we receive the gift of having them pointed out. Our perspectives on race, class, gender, and sexuality necessarily arise from our particular context and story. Just as it's valuable and sometimes lifesaving to have a blind spot pointed out while we're driving, the same is true in our everyday lives. We need one another to truly see.

Becoming Connective Tissue

As these collective relationships across places grow in curiosity, encouragement, and solidarity, we begin to grow in trust (see fig. 8.2). This is how we can strengthen the tenuous fabric of care that's so critical for our common life.

Our neighbors, our institutions, and even our democratic system need significant help. Whether we call it "the fractured republic," as Yuval Levin has discussed, or the "unwinding," as documented by George Packer, our neighborhoods, cities, and nations need collaborative, ground-up repair.[9] As we create relationships of trust across neighborhoods, we are literally at the ground level fighting against the storm of individualism and polarization that is ripping us apart.

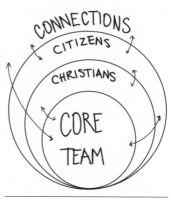

Figure 8.2. The connective tissue

While each of us as individuals will have our part to play, if the local church is able to lean deeply into its calling as a reconciling and restoring force, we should embrace the truth that we need communities learning how to collaborate with other communities. As we learn from one another, as we share our stories, we will begin to uncover just how much we truly need one another.

Unfortunately, the majority of the campaigns seeking to educate and inspire us to take action are aimed at individuals on behalf of one particular issue. These campaigns are important and needed, but they will never get us where we need to be. Whether the campaign is to strengthen families, fight human trafficking, start social enterprises, or disrupt the school-to-prison pipeline, needed beneath all of these crucial issues is a community of care that's present in a very real place.

Without grounded communities that care about their whole place, who are seeking the shalom of everyone and everything there, we may inadvertently find ourselves competing for attention and budgets when we should be collaborating in our shared proximity. Please don't hear me wrong. We need expert guidance on these crucial matters, but if we are not looking to cultivate communities whose primary task is learning how it all fits together, then we will be competing for time and money.

When communities that are embedded in the story of a real place learn from others in the same position, these issues are not sidestepped. Instead, they take on real flesh and blood; they happen in real buildings in real places and are affected by real neighbors. We don't need to keep sheltering ourselves from the reality of injustice—that's a practical heresy. We need to listen for how we can show up in the lives of real people who are deeply embedded in our broken systems and learn how to work from there. When these relationships are in place, experts and campaigns can be leveraged for massive transformation.

Some might think it's not such a big deal to connect one neighborhood to another. It might feel like a nice add-on to the real work of presence in our places. But I'm convinced it's the primary path of healing—as long as we also remain deeply rooted.

We need to reclaim the reality that building trust, naming blind spots, and discerning the next steps together are not just for us. Rev. Jennifer Bailey wisely says, "Relationships move at the speed of trust: social change moves at the speed of relationships."[10] Just as we seek to step back and discern God's dreams when we gather in our own places, we need to help one another see what is possible in the places we visit. There is nothing cute about this. This is not an adorable little sideshow while the real grown-ups are doing the hard work in places like the United Nations in New York, the banking district of London, or the World Economic Forum in Davos, Switzerland. When we stitch together relationships of trust among embedded communities whose primary orientation is toward

God's dream, we are simultaneously knitting together a network that can reimagine capitalism as we know it, transform democracy at the local level, and reconstruct how we build our neighborhoods and cities.

There is no single issue that would not benefit from a growing network of churches who take responsibility for their patch of ground in a holistic manner. The tragedies of mass incarceration, the broken adoption system, faltering public schools, the growing opioid crisis, homelessness, and gentrification, to name just a few, are deeply interconnected. These very complex and persistent problems will not be solved one at a time. We will be able to confront these issues only within a network that is able to learn from itself, take action where it is, and continue to trust God's work at the end of the day. This is what's at stake. Whenever we hear people being anxious about the future of the church, we must reframe the conversation toward this end. It's not about preserving nostalgia or refusing to grieve for the "golden era" when our pews were overflowing with people. It is about reclaiming our baptism into the revolution that is the kingdom of God on earth as it is in heaven.

Practices

The following are three practices for communities to listen to and learn from other communities. Obviously, this is not exhaustive, but starting here is better than not starting at all. We simply cannot fathom what God can do with us when we learn how to be deeply interwoven into the lives of our neighborhood and learn from others across town, across the country, and across the world.

Take a road trip. Parents and grandparents know the sense of instant connection when other people take good care of their kids. When we feel that someone really cares about our children, it's hard not to have an instant bond with them. I think the same is true of our neighborhoods. When a small team visits and asks good questions, cares about what is happening, and celebrates what the neighbors have sought to achieve, the natural result is growing trust between their communities. I have been in hundreds of neighborhoods with groups small and large and can honestly say I've been inspired every single time. It's a gift to host a few new friends and receive their encouragement, and it's a gift to see what others are doing. Take a walk. Meet others in pubs or coffee shops. Ask people for stories of how God is at work. By doing this we will be inspired and help remind one another how to keep the main thing the main thing. Think about another community in your city or state that you know cares about what God is doing in their neighborhood, and invite them to use their fresh eyes to help you see more clearly what God might be doing in yours. Ask them if you could come for a visit. You'll be astounded at what can transpire as you walk your neighborhood with new friends.

Invite honest feedback. Once there is a bit more trust built up between communities, it's wise to go a little deeper and ask for their honest thoughts. Remember, we aren't inviting experts for their assessment; these are not our bosses. If you invite a few friends or leaders from another neighborhood to explore with you, you'll be talking with peers. Obviously, they will ask different questions, observe different dynamics, and be interested in different story lines. All of these inquiries can be helpful. This way of being the church is endlessly complex; there are no easy formulas that tell us what to do. Wisdom and discernment will always be needed. Receiving these insights from fellow practitioners, especially when you have gotten to know each other, is healthy. It will always be up to your community to determine what to do with the feedback and questions, but hearing from these friends can save untold amounts of heartbreak and open up all sorts of new ideas.

Celebrate together. When the time is right, we need to learn how to champion each other. At the heart of every Parish Collective conference or story night is the desire to celebrate these everyday stories of faithful presence. It would be amazing if this work was already happening in denominations, seminaries, and foundations. Someday that will be normal, but right now it's not the case. We need to figure out how to make a big deal out of one another. We need to keep reminding ourselves that our ordinary acts of love and care are big stuff from God's perspective. Don't listen to the noise. Instead, learn how to come together in church buildings, community centers, concert halls, and even arenas to raise our voices of gratitude and lament to God; let him know where we are depending on God to act. There is something magical about being together with dozens, hundreds, or even thousands of friends who are each seeking to join God in loving their places well. By knitting this web of care across neighborhoods, let's keep telling our stories well and celebrating each other with every chance we can get.

POSTSCRIPT

Without Ceasing

*To clasp the hands in prayer is the beginning
of an uprising against the disorder of the world.*

KARL BARTH

The common thread in everything written in this book, everything hoped for, every challenge named, is the need for prayer.

Nothing discussed here is possible if we are not dependent on God. When we pray, we are putting ourselves in the correct posture that says we can't control the outcomes we seek. When we pray, we have already sought to "wait on the Lord" because we have acknowledged we are powerless to bring about the transformation we seek. When we pray, we follow the lead of the earliest church, which put its patient trust in God despite overwhelming adversity.

May the posture and practice of prayer be in our listening, our speaking, our lamenting, our praising, and our groaning without words for the dreams of God to emerge into the fabric of our actual lives. And when we pray, let's remember that we are not alone.

ACKNOWLEDGMENTS

This book is the direct result of the inspiration, grit, and resilience of the ordinary saints I've been privileged to meet through the Parish Collective. I could not be more grateful for each and every one I've met. I'm convinced a movement is well underway thanks to you.

Paul Sparks, thank you for embodying the soul of this movement.

Christiana Rice, thank you for your audacious leap of faith.

Dwight Friesen, Jonathan Brooks, Gideon Tsang, Kate Pattison, Eileen Suico, and Kirk Lauckner, thank you for your embodied wisdom and crucial support.

Don Jacobson, thank you for believing in me and in this project.

Ethan McCarthy, thank you for taking the risk you took in your feedback and your keen editorial eye.

My parents, Dave and Jane, thank you for your unwavering support and steady investment of prayer.

Most especially to my wife, Coté: your courageous love for me, our boys, and our neighborhood is a constant inspiration. Thank you for showing me the way.

NOTES

1 The Movement or the Meltdown

[1]Margot Adler, "Before Rosa Parks, There Was Claudette Colvin," *NPR*, March 15, 2009, www.npr.org/2009/03/15/101719889/before-rosa-parks -there-was-claudette-colvin.

[2]George Packer, *The Unwinding: An Inner History of the New America* (New York: Farrar, Straus and Giroux, 2013).

2 The Big Why

[1]Simon Sinek, *Start with Why* (New York: Penguin, 2011), 70.

[2]Fleming Rutledge, *Advent: The Once and Future Coming of Jesus Christ* (Grand Rapids: Eerdmans, 2018), 13.

[3]Howard Snyder, *Salvation Means Creation Healed* (Eugene, OR: Wipf & Stock, 2011), 65.

[4]Bernard Van Der Kolk, *The Body Keeps the Score: Brain, Mind, and Body in the Healing of Trauma* (New York: Penguin, 2015).

[5]Wendell Berry, *It All Turns on Affection: The Jefferson Lecture and Other Essays* (Berkeley, CA: Counterpoint, 2012), 9.

[6]James K. A. Smith, *You Are What You Love* (Grand Rapids: Brazos, 2016).

3 The Magic of Paying Attention

[1]Paul Lewis, "'Our Minds Can Be Hijacked': The Tech Insiders Who Fear a Smartphone Dystopia," *Guardian*, October 6, 2017, www.theguardian.com /technology/2017/oct/05/smartphone-addiction-silicon-valley-dystopia.

[2]Simon Parkin, "Has Dopamine Got Us Hooked on Tech?" *Guardian*, March 4, 2018, www.theguardian.com/technology/2018/mar/04/has -dopamine-got-us-hooked-on-tech-facebook-apps-addiction.

[3]Justin Rosenstein, quoted in Lewis, "'Our Minds Can Be Hijacked.'"

[4]"Technology Isn't Only Hijacking Our Time, It's Controlling Our Choices," *Aspen Ideas to Go*, June 12, 2019, www.aspeninstitute.org /podcasts/technology-isnt-only-hijacking-our-time-its-controlling-our -choices.

[5]Paul Sparks, Tim Soerens, and Dwight J. Friesen, *The New Parish* (Downers Grove, IL: InterVarsity Press, 2014), 57.

[6]Charles Taylor, *A Secular Age* (Cambridge, MA: Belknap Press, 2007), 593.

[7]José Humphreys, *Seeing Jesus in East Harlem* (Downers Grove, IL: Inter-Varsity Press, 2018), 150

[8]Peter Block (keynote address, Conspire Gathering, North Church, Cincinnati, October 12, 2018).

[9]See, for example, Willie James Jennings, *The Christian Imagination: Theology and Origins of Race* (New Haven, CT: Yale University Press, 2010); Lamin Sanneh, *Whose Religion Is Christianity: The Gospel Beyond the West* (Grand Rapids: Eerdmans, 2003); James H. Evans Jr., *We Have Been Believers: An African American Systemic Theology* (Minneapolis: Fortress Press, 2012); and Diana Butler Bass, *A People's History of Christianity* (San Francisco: HarperOne, 2010).

[10]Willie James Jennings, *Acts*, Belief: A Theological Commentary on the Bible (Louisville, KY: John Knox Press, 2017), 2.

[11]"About," *Brené Brown*, accessed January 17, 2020, www.brenebrown.com.

4 *The Megachurch Next Door*

[1]Attributed to Archbishop William Temple (1881–1944).

[2]Marshall McLuhan, *Understanding the Media: The Extensions of Man*, repr. ed. (Cambridge, MA: MIT Press, 1994), 7.

[3]Shannan Martin, *The Ministry of Ordinary Places: Waking Up to God's Goodness All Around You* (Nashville: Thomas Nelson, 2018), 18.

[4]Lesslie Newbigin, *The Household of God: Lectures on the Nature of the Church* (Eugene, OR: Wipf & Stock, 2008), 27.

5 *The Parish Is the Unit of Change*

[1]David Brooks, "The Neighborhood Is the Unit of Change," *New York Times*, October 10, 2018, www.nytimes.com/2018/10/18/opinion/neighborhood -social-infrastructure-community.html.

[2]Paul Sparks, Tim Soerens, and Dwight J. Friesen, *The New Parish* (Downers Grove, IL, InterVarsity Press, 2014), 23.

[3]Sparks, Soerens, and Friesen, *New Parish*, 23.

[4]See, for example, Geoffrey Holsclaw, "Is Babel Reversed at Pentecost?" Northern Seminary, May 26, 2015, www.seminary.edu/is-babel-reversed -at-pentecost.

[5]David Brooks, *The Second Mountain: The Quest for a Moral Life* (New York: Random House, 2019), xvii.

[6]Andy Crouch, *Culture Making: Recovering Our Creative Calling* (Downers Grove, IL: InterVarsity Press, 2013), 67.

[7]John McKnight, "Reflections from John McKnight" (speech, Nebraska Community Foundation Conference, Lincoln, NE, January 5, 2015).

[8]The following movements are explained in more detail in chap. 6 of Sparks, Soerens, and Friesen, *New Parish*.

[9]This insight came in conversation with Dan prompted by JR Woodward and Dan White Jr., *Church as Movement: Starting and Sustaining Missional-Incarnational Communities* (Downers Grove, IL: InterVarsity Press, 2016).

[10]Tish Warren, *Liturgy of the Ordinary: Sacred Practices in Everyday Life* (Downers Grove, IL: InterVarsity Press, 2016), 21.

6 The Same Team

[1]Ashley Ross, "The Long History Behind Ash Wednesday Traditions," *Time*, February 10, 2016, https://time.com/4210001/ash-wednesday-ash -forehead.

[2]"Lutheranism by Region," Wikipedia, accessed December 18, 2019, https://en.wikipedia.org/wiki/Lutheranism_by_region; and Jennifer Powell McNutt, "Division Is Not Always a Scandal," *Christianity Today*, December 30, 2016, www.christianitytoday.com/ct/2017/january-february /division-is-not-always-scandal.html.

[3]David Schnarch, *Passionate Marriage* (New York, W. W. Norton, 2009), 140.

[4]"First Differentiation-based Approach to Marital and Sexual Therapy," *Crucible Therapy*, accessed December 18, 2019, https://crucibletherapy.com /approach-marital-sexual-therapy.

[5]Jonathan Brooks, *Church Forsaken: Practicing Presence in Neglected Neighborhoods* (Downers Grove, IL: InterVarsity Press, 2018), 57.

7 *Learning from Local Heroes*

[1]Peter Wohlleben, *The Hidden Life of Trees: What They Feel, How They Communicate; Discoveries from a Secret World* (Vancouver, BC: Greystone Books, 2016), 8.

[2]Gerard Helferich, "The Wood-Wide Web," *Wall Street Journal*, September 30, 2016, https://www.wsj.com/articles/the-hidden-life-of-trees-peter-wohlleben-1475167885.

[3]James Fallows and Deborah Fallows, *Our Towns: A 100,000-mile Journey into the Heart of America* (New York: Pantheon, 2019), 12.

[4]Cormac Russell, "Sustainable Community Development: From What's Wrong to What's Strong," TEDxExeter, May 16, 2016, www.youtube.com/watch?v=a5xR4QB1Adw.

[5]Tim Keller, *Every Good Endeavor: Connecting Your Work to God's Work* (New York: Penguin, 2014), 194.

[6]"The Shadow Proves the Sunshine," track 4 on Switchfoot, *Nothing Is Sound*, Sony BMG Music Entertainment, 2005.

[7]Michael Mather, *Having Nothing, Possessing Everything: Finding Abundant Communities in Unexpected Places* (Grand Rapids: Eerdmans, 2018), 34.

[8]Cathleen Falsani, "Bono's American Prayer," *Christianity Today*, February 21, 2003, www.christianitytoday.com/ct/2003/marchweb-only/2.38.html.

8 *Already Here*

[1]Albert Schweitzer, quoted in Marie Dalton, Dawn G. Hoyle, and Marie W. Watts, *Human Relations* (Boston: Cengage Learning, 2010), 234.

[2]"Things that are accepted now": Seth Godin, "How Idea Adoption Works—The Idea Progression," *Seth's Blog*, September 10, 2015, https://seths.blog/2015/09/how-idea-adoption-works-the-idea-progression.

[3]Geoffrey A. Moore, *Crossing the Chasm* (New York: Harper Business, 2014).

[4]Alan Kreider, *The Patient Ferment of the Early Church* (Grand Rapids: Baker Academic, 2016).

[5] Andy2i, "The Power of Compounding: $1 Million Now or Penny Doubling for a Month," *Saving2Invest*, accessed January 22, 2020, www.savingtoinvest.com/power-of-compounding-1-million-now-or.

[6]Steven Johnson, "Where Good Ideas Come From," *TED Global 2010*, accessed December 19, 2019, https://www.ted.com/talks/steven_johnson_where_good_ideas_come_from.html;/discussion#t-242225.

[7]Michael Polanyi, *The Tacit Dimension* (Chicago: University of Chicago Press, 2009), 4.

[8]Since I travel a fair amount for work, this book was written in a few different countries and quite a few different cities. While I wrote this section, I was in Oakland, California, and texted my wife. I gave her my list of how superwhite I am and asked for any more suggestions. Within seconds she replied, "IPA," which I was drinking at the exact time of our conversation.

[9]See Yuval Levin, *The Fractured Republic: Renewing America's Social Contract in the Age of Individualism* (New York: Basic Books, 2016); and George Packer, *The Unwinding: An Inner History of the New America* (New York: Farrar, Straus and Giroux, 2013).

[10]Jennifer Bailey, quoted in Krista Tippett, "Jennifer Bailey and Lennon Flowers: An Invitation to Brave Space," *On Being* (blog), October 17, 2019, https://onbeing.org/programs/jennifer-bailey-and-lennon-flowers-an -invitation-to-brave-space.

PARISH COLLECTIVE
GROW ROOTS. WEAVE LINKS.

Join thousands of creative practitioners around the globe learning to collaborate together in, with, and for the neighborhood.

✦ Discover all the people of faith who care about the neighborhood the way you do.

✦ Connect to other churches and groups through a guided peer-learning community.

✦ Celebrate the insights of the collective with a story night or conference near you.

WWW.PARISHCOLLECTIVE.ORG

IVP PRAXIS

EQUIPPING LEADERS FOR MINISTRY

"...TO EQUIP HIS PEOPLE FOR WORKS OF SERVICE,
SO THAT THE BODY OF CHRIST MAY BE BUILT UP."

EPHESIANS 4:12

God has called us to ministry. But it's not enough to have a vision for ministry if you don't have the practical skills for it. Nor is it enough to do the work of ministry if what you do is headed in the wrong direction. We need both vision *and* expertise for effective ministry. We need *praxis*.

Praxis puts theory into practice. It brings cutting-edge ministry expertise from visionary practitioners. You'll find sound biblical and theological foundations for ministry in the real world, with concrete examples for effective action and pastoral ministry. Praxis books are more than the "how to" – they're also the "why to." And because *being* is every bit as important as *doing*, Praxis attends to the inner life of the leader as well as the outer work of ministry. Feed your soul, and feed your ministry.

If you are called to ministry, you know you can't do it on your own. Let Praxis provide the companions you need to equip God's people for life in the kingdom.

www.ivpress.com/praxis